IELTS
PRACTICE TESTS:

IELTS General Training Book with 140 Reading, Writing, Speaking & Vocabulary Test Prep Questions for the IELTS Exam

© 2018 Trellis Test Prep

All rights reserved. The contents of this book, or any part thereof, may not be reprinted or reproduced in any manner whatsoever without written permission from the publisher.

Printed in the United States of America

Contents

Introduction	7
Listening Questions	9
Reading Questions	31
Structure & Expression Questions	53
Writing Essay Question	63
Listening Answers	67
Reading Answers	93
Structure & Expression Answers	119
Writing Essay Answers	133

Introduction

The International English Language Testing System (IELTS) is a required literacy test that measures the ability of non-native speakers who would like to attend English-speaking educational institutions or be employed by English-speaking businesses. But that doesn't mean it should be difficult!

The IELTS Practice Tests from Trellis Test Prep offers the strategies and tips to help you pass the IELTS exam. By mirroring exactly what you'll see on the IELTS test, the IELTS study guide will help you understand the format and types of practice questions you'll be expected to know on test day.

Trellis Test Prep collaborates with tutors and educational experts for our IELTS practice test prep book, which includes the following:

- IELTS Vocabulary
- IELTS Words
- IELTS Reading
- IELTS Writing

- IELTS Speaking
- IELTS Listening
- IELTS Grammar

Listening Questions

LISTENING

Directions: The listening section evaluates your capacity to understand conversations and lectures in English. In this section, you will hear several short conversations and answer questions about these conversations. The questions frequently ask about the main idea and supporting details. Sometimes the questions ask about the speaker's purpose or attitude. Always answer the questions using what is said or implied by the speakers.

Most questions are worth one point. If the question is worth more, it will be stated in the directions.

During the actual test, you will be able to take notes and use the notes to answer the questions. Your notes will not be evaluated.

Part 1

(Female speaker) I recently studied a paper on morphology for my teacher's certificate. Morphology is so hard. My teacher was really great though. He made morphology interesting and tied it to different languages. Even so, I didn't understand a lot of the class and I hated it.

1. What did the woman say made the class easier to understand?

   A. The professor
   B. The paper was easy to understand
   C. Her teaching background
   D. Her ability to understand other languages

2. Which sentence best expresses what the woman means when she says:
   He made morphology interesting and <u>tied it</u> to different languages.

   A. fixed it to other morphologies
   B. connected it to other languages
   C. explained it in the student's native language
   D. explained morphology in terms the woman could understand

(Male student) Last night I watched the soccer match between Portugal and France. Everyone expected France to win, but Portugal won in the last seconds of the game. What a surprise! I have never seen a game I enjoyed more.

3. What was the man doing last night?

   A. Enjoying a football game
   B. Watching an exciting soccer game
   C. Watching his favorite team
   D. Enjoying a relaxing soccer game

(Male student) Tomorrow I am going to the soccer stadium to watch our team defeat their opponents. I know we will win because we have the best team. Even though, we have several injuries, three of our players are going to the Olympics, and one of the players won the best player award last year.

4. Why does the man believe that his team is the best *team? Choose 2 answers.*

   A. Three players are going to the Olympics
   B. Their keeper has the fewest goals scored against him
   C. Several of their players are injured.
   D. Last year, one of their players was the best player.

(Male student) I have backpacked around Europe before and never had any problems. Traveling by yourself forces you to try to communicate with the local people. It's a great way to meet people you wouldn't if you were traveling with friends. I like to carry a small notebook with me to write my observations in when I was eating alone in a small café or restaurant. Most of the time, I would talk to other diners and forget my notebook. Traveling alone is great because you can do whatever you want to and you don't have to do what the group is doing. There are two big drawbacks however. One is it can be more expensive. It's cheaper when you share a room with a friend. Sometimes, it gets lonely. Still, I think you should try it.

5. What is the main idea of the paragraph?

A. The man recommends traveling in a group.
B. The man likes to travel alone.
C. The man feels that traveling alone is more expensive.
D. The man thinks traveling with a small group of friends is better.

6. According to the man, what all of the following are reasons to travel alone EXCEPT.

A. Sometimes, it gets lonely if you travel by yourself.
B. You can do whatever the group wants to do.
C. It is cheaper when you share a room.
D. You meet more people.

(Female student) People forget their cell phones and wash them. I have had this happen to two different friends. One dropped her cell phone in the washing machine by accident. The other one didn't know her cell phone was in the back pocket of her jeans. They both tried to dry the phones out by using rice, but they were not successful. I thought these stories were so funny, but they were really expensive mistakes.

7. Why did the people wash their cell phones?

   A. It was a class assignment.
   B. They were experimenting.
   C. They were funny jokes.
   D. They were expensive mistakes.

8. Why did the women put their phones in rice?

   A. They wanted to cook the rice.
   B. They believed the rice would dry the phones out.
   C. They thought that the rice would make the phones work again.
   D. They wanted the rice to neutralize the soap in the phone.

(Female student) My professor recently began using podcasts for our classes. She believes that her students like the newer technologies so much that they pay more attention to the podcasts than the textbook. Her philosophy is "If you can't lick them, join them".

I really like the idea of podcasts, but I don't know if I am going to like them if we have to study using them.

9. What does the woman's professor mean when she says "if you can't lick them, join them"?

   A. The professor means that you can't win if you continue to do the same things the same way.
   B. The professor means that you should try something new.
   C. The professor means that you must join others if they won't join you.
   D. The professor means that it is better to do what the students want to do.

10. What can we infer is the reason the woman is uncertain she will like podcasts as part of her classes?

   A. The woman probably believes that the podcasts will be boring.
   B. The woman likes podcasts now, but she is afraid that they will be uninteresting later on.
   C. The woman believes that podcasts should be for her personal use, not study time.
   D. The professor has required her students to watch lots of podcasts.

(Female Student) Last weekend, I overheard my little sister talking on her cell phone with her best friend. She was telling her friend not to say anything to my mother about her grades in school. I think my sister is getting a bad grade in history or algebra. Those are her worst two subjects. My mother gets very upset when we don't get good grades. If I tell my mother, my sister may tell on me another time.

11. Why is the woman upset that she overheard the conversation?

   A. She is afraid that her friend will tell her mother something bad about her.
   B. She is worried about her little sister's chemistry grades.
   C. She believes that her sister may be getting bad grades in school.
   D. She feels like she has to keep the secret about the bad grades in history also.

12. Why is the woman worried about her mother's reaction?

   A. Because her mother doesn't like for the girls to get bad grades.
   B. Because her mother wants the girls to get home earlier.
   C. Because her mother will say they must study more.
   D. Because her mother punish them.

(Female speaker) One time when I was babysitting, I started getting cold, so I turned up the heat. I still didn't get warm, so I turned it up some more. I remember when the parents came in; they thought it was really hot in the house. I guess I was still cold, because I was so still.

13. Why does the woman turn up the heat the second time?

    A. She was hot.
    B. She was feverish.
    C. She was still cold.
    D. She was ill.

14. Why was the woman still cold?

    A. She was not moving.
    B. She was getting sick.
    C. The house was cold.
    D. The parents were cold, too.

(Male student) I am just learning to use my smart phone as a GPS device. I have had some funny experiences. One time, I put in the address wrong. I typed in the number for one address, but the street name for another. Instead of going to my dentist's new office, I wound up at a house being demolished. I guess I'll have to be more careful in the future.

15. According to the man, what advice does he give about using GPS devices?

    A. He thinks these devices are a waste of time.
    B. He believes that they are great for most people.
    C. He believes if you aren't careful, you could have problems.
    D. He suggests using them only when you need them.

16. Why did the man go to a house being demolished?

    A. He didn't know how to use his phone.
    B. He was unfamiliar with GPS devices.
    C. He put in the wrong address.
    D. He was looking for a new address.

(Male student) Our teacher was explaining about different sleeping habits of people. Many people like to get up early and feel really good in the morning, but not me. I am a night owl. I don't really get going until about 6 P.M. She told us that a lot of people prefer to take power naps. She is a morning person, but she takes power naps, too. If I took a power nap, I would be so grouchy that no one could stand me!

17. What is the text mainly about?

    A. The man's sleep habits.
    B. The teachers sleeping habits.
    C. Different sleeping habits of people.
    D. The way we adjust to sleep.

18. What can we infer that "power naps" means?
    A. A short period of sleep
    B. A rejuvenating period of sleep
    C. A long sleep before bedtime
    D. A short, refreshing period of sleep

19. What does the man mean when he says "I would be so grouchy that no one could stand me?"

    A. that he would be happy.
    B. That he would be cross.
    C. That he would be sleepy.
    D. That he would be wide awake.

(Male student) I am studying to be a doctor. My parents have always wanted me to be one. I like science, and I like to help people. We are just beginning to interact with patients, and I am really good at listening to them, but you know what? I would really like to be a chef. Boy it would really upset my parents if I gave up medical school to cook in our restaurant.

20. What does the man say he would like to be?

    A. A patient
    B. A chef
    C. A doctor
    D. A scientist

21. What can we infer his parents do?

    A. They work in their restaurant.
    B. They are doctors.
    C. They work in medicine.
    D. They are teachers.

22. Why does the man believe he is good with patients?

    A. He likes science.
    B. He likes to talk with people.
    C. He is a good listener.
    D. He gets good grades in med school.

(Female student) My mom went to a convention in Albuquerque last week. She loved all the activities at the convention, but she was not well while she was there. First of all, she had to go up and down stairs a lot for the different presentations, so her knees hurt. Secondly, she had difficulty breathing. Since she is usually very healthy, she thought it was because of the high altitude.

(Male student) I know. In Mexico City, where I am from, is over 7,000 feet high. Sometimes, tourists get altitude sickness. It usually passes in a few days, but at first, it can be difficult to breathe.

23. Why did the woman's mother have difficulty breathing?

    A. Because Mexico City was very high.
    B. Because Albuquerque has a high altitude.
    C. Because she had to go downstairs for presentations.
    D. Because she has health problems.

24. When tourists get altitude sickness, all of the following happen EXCEPT

    A. It usually lasts several days.
    B. It causes breathing problems.
    C. They feel a little sick.
    D. They love all the activities.

25. Why did the woman's mother have problems with the presentations?

    A. She had to listen really well.
    B. She had difficulty hearing the speakers.
    C. She had problems with her headphones.
    D. She had to go up and down stairs.

(Female student) Yesterday, I visited my grandma. I can't believe how old-fashioned she is. She didn't like my pink hair. I explained it was a fashion statement, not a true color. And then, she hated my tattoos. I only have three small tattoos: a dolphin on the back of my neck, a heart on my ankle and a butterfly on my wrist. She said that I would be sorry I had colored my skin with permanent ink because fashion comes and goes. Lucky for me, I had removed my nose ring, or she would have really been upset.

26. Why was the grandmother upset with her granddaughter?

    A. Because she didn't like the haircut.
    B. Because she didn't like tattoos the granddaughter chose.
    C. Because she had too many tattoos.
    D. Because the tattoos were permanent.

27. Why does the woman imply that her grandmother is old-fashioned?

    A. Because she doesn't like unusual hair colors.
    B. Because she the tattoos are of unpleasant objects.
    C. Because the grandmother didn't like her granddaughter's fashions.
    D. Because the grandmother has pink hair and tattoos on her ankle.

(Female student) I have decided to become a vegetarian. I am not going to eat meat anymore. I really enjoy rice, beans, vegetables, and fruits, so why should I continue to eat meat? Sometimes, I get ill if I eat meat or chicken. I believe that animals deserve to live, too. I may become a vegan later on, but right now, I plan to still eat eggs and cheese. They are two of my favorite foods. And you can make a quiche with them.

28. Why is the woman becoming a vegetarian?

    A. Because she likes eggs and cheese.
    B. Because she likes vegetables.
    C. Because she doesn't like meat.
    D. Because of her health.

29. According to the text, what foods do vegetarians eat that vegans don't eat?

    A. Rice and beans
    B. Vegetables and fruits
    C. Cheese and eggs
    D. Fruits

30. What are the woman's two favorite foods?

    A. Fruits and vegetables
    B. Vegetables and eggs
    C. Cheese and rice
    D. Cheese and eggs

LISTENING

Part 2

(CONVERSATION TRANSCRIPT)

(NARRATOR) Listen to a conversation between a female student and a male student and then answer the questions.

(Female student) Hi, James. Did you see the soccer game on TV yesterday?

(Male student) No. I had a lot of studying to do for the finals in chemistry. I prefer bicycle riding to soccer anyway.

(Female student) You do? I thought everyone liked soccer.

(Male student) I like soccer and basketball, but I prefer riding bicycles. What did you do over the weekend?

(Female student) Well, I had to work. My new boss is really demanding. She wants us all to know all the items on the menu and to keep the restaurant spotless.

(Male student) That's really great. You are getting good experience in the restaurant business.

(Female student) I know. The problem is when we are very busy; it's hard to remember everything. I started last summer so I know the menu pretty well, but it is hard with so many changes at once.

(Male student) What's your favorite food?

(Female student) Me? I like everything. I love tacos, spaghetti, pizza, and fried chicken. That's Mexican, Italian, and United States food. What a mixture.

(Male student) Wow, it's like the United States population. The people come here from so many different places. I guess they bring their favorite foods with them.

(Female student) I know. My parents came from Colombia. Their favorite food is beans and rice. They love to fry ripe plantains to go with them, and I love the flan they serve for dessert.

(Male student) Plantains? What are these things? What is flan?

(Female student giggling) Well, plantains are large bananas that must be cooked before you eat them. Flan is a baked custard or pudding made with eggs and milk. My mom makes it with caramel syrup. She turns it upside-down and cools it in the refrigerator for several hours or overnight. It is heaven in your mouth. So cold and creamy.

(Male student) Sounds good. Hey. Have you heard about the highways being widened in front of the university? That is going to cause so many problems for us coming to school.

(Female student) Why?

(Male student) Because the exits will be narrower and fewer during construction. It will be impossible to get to school quickly. We will have to get up earlier and leave home earlier.

(Female student) Not me. I walk to school, remember?

(Male student) Oh, yeah. I forgot. I've got to go. My test starts on the dot at 10.

(Female student) Hey, you better get going. It's a quarter until 10 right now.

1. What are the speakers mainly discussing?

A. How the woman should prepare for her class.
B. The woman's responsibilities at home.
C. The plans to widen the highway near the school.
D. Different events of everyday life.

2. Who is difficult for the female speaker to please?

A. The male speaker
B. Her boss
C. Her parents
D. Her mom

3. There are two answers for the next question. *Mark the two answers.*

Why does the male speaker believe that the widening of the highway will cause difficulties for him to get to school?

A. The roads will be narrower.
B. There will be more traffic.
C. There will be many bicycles on the roads.
D. There will be fewer exits.

4. Read part of the conversation again. Then answer the question.

   (Male student) Oh, yeah. I forgot. I've got to go. My test starts on the dot at 10.

   What does the man mean when he says: 'on the dot at 10?

A. The test begins around 10.
B. The test begins precisely at 10.
C. The test will start as soon as the students arrive for their 10 class.
D. The test at approximately 10 o'clock.

5. Why does the man mean when he says: 'we will have to get up earlier and leave home earlier'?

A. It will take him longer to travel to school because of traffic police.
B. The roads will be more congested because of more exits.
C. He expects the next year's classes to begin earlier.
D. The man thinks construction will cause traffic delays.

6. According to the text, what is flan?

A. A cooked banana.
B. An appetizer.
C. A dessert.
D. Heaven in your mouth

7. What does the man's favorite sport?

   A. Soccer
   B. Football
   C. Cycling
   D. Basketball

8. Why does the woman find it difficult to do her job at the restaurant well?

   A. Because her boss is very demanding.
   B. Because she has a poor memory.
   C. Because the boss is always complaining.
   D. Because they get very busy at times.

LISTENING

Part 3

(Narrator) Listen to part of a lecture in a science class.

(Male professor) Today I'm going to talk about the small world of machines. In the past, machines were unable to work at a micro- (or tiny) scale. For example, doctors did not have tools that allowed them to repair the body from the inside. Plumbers did not have any way to locate broken pipes deep inside a building. Now, things are changing. Computers and biophysics are creating a new world where scientists can build microscopic machines. This is the exciting world of nanotechnology.

Just look at some of the uses of nanotechnology.

- A probe that provides images of a patient's arteries is being used in cardiology centers around the world.
- A product which uses nanoparticles to clean glass by breaking down dirt particles and wash them away when water comes in contact with the glass.
- Clothing that contains a thin layer of zinc oxide to protect against UV radiation.
- Scratch resistant polymer coatings that contain aluminum silicate nanoparticles making earlier polymer coatings more effective by increasing resistance to chipping and scratching.
- Bandages that incorporate nanoparticles of silver ions to block harmful bacteria's ability to breath.

Nanotechnology is producing new products every day. Many exciting medical applications have been invented, but nanotechnology isn't limited to the field of medicine. In the world of tennis, Wilson has created a tennis ball with a double core. The inner core has a coating of clay nanoparticles that makes it very difficult for air to escape from the ball. The tennis racket has been engineered with nanotube-infused graphite. This creates a very light racket many times stronger than steel.

Yet, all of these advances have challenges and risks, too. Scientists need to learn more about how atoms join together to create larger structures. On a smaller scale, a nanoscale, elements act differently than in larger groups. Some scientists believe that nanoparticles could be dangerous to humans even toxic. They fear that the nanoparticles could pass from the bloodstream into the brain.

Tomorrow's lecture will concern the ethics of nanotechnology. Is it ethical to create a race of humans that are enhanced by nanotechnology? Is it ethical to build stronger and more lethal weapons? What will happen to manufacturing jobs if nanotechnology eliminates the need for them? These are just some of the questions we will discuss in tomorrow's class.

[**SOURCE:** Bonsor, K & Strickland, J. How Nanotechnology Works. http://science.howstuffworks.com/nanotechnology.htm]

1. What is the lecture mainly about?

A. Innovations in nanotechnology
B. A comparison of nanotechnology and previous technology.
C. The ethics of nanotechnology
D. Problems with nanotechnology.

2. In what way is nanotechnology different from previous technology?

A. It is smaller.
B. It is microscopic.
C. It is larger.
D. It is huge.

3. According to the professor, which one of the following options is an actual nanotechnology product in use today?

A. Clothing that can wash itself.
B. Bandages that kill bacteria by eliminating their food source.
C. Scratch-proof paint for cars.
D. Glass that can clean itself.

4. In his next class, the professor will lecture about all of the following EXCEPT

   A. Creating a new race of humans
   B. The economics of nanotechnology
   C. The ethics of more lethal weapons
   D. The need for smaller medical devices

Listen to the following presentation by a school guidance counselor. Then, answer the questions.

Good morning. I wanted to talk to you about applying for the college or university of your choice. There are many factors to be considered.

First of all, your grades are very important. Many colleges won't even consider new students with poor grades. However, if your tests, such as the IELTS, are very good, then they will compare your grades and the tests to make a decision.

Secondly, your after school activities are important. These are important because they show what your interests are when you can choose what you want to do. The admissions officers want to know if you worked or gave your time to help others. Were you interested in sports?

Finally, there're scholarships. Sometimes, if you are very good in sports, any sport, you might be eligible for a sports scholarship. However, sports scholarships aren't the only ones available. There are scholarships for almost anything you want to study: chemistry, English, and even, home economics. There are scholarships for the children of certain ethnic groups and for the children of previous students of the institution.

To conclude, I want to invite you to set up an appointment with me to discuss your options. My office is open from 8 – 10 for short questions like setting up appointments. I try to keep the afternoon hours open for longer appointments, but come to see me. We will work something out; I try to accommodate everyone.

Thank you for your attention.

5. What is the main idea of the talk?

   A. The counselor wants everyone to go to college.
   B. The counselor is discussing the factors college admissions officer study use in the admissions process.
   C. Factors to be considered in applying to college.
   D. How to get a scholarship

6. What does the counselor say is the most import factor in the admissions process?

   A. Grades
   B. Scholarships
   C. Test scores
   D. Sports

7. Part of the conversation is repeated below. Read it and answer the question.

   We will work something out; I try to accommodate everyone.

What does the counselor mean by this statement?

   A. She is flexible and will try to adjust her schedule to the student's.
   B. She will help the student get into college.
   C. She tries to make appointments for all the school personnel.
   D. She wants to be helpful.

8. According to the presentation, what does the counselor say about scholarships? *Choose 2 answers.*
   A. Many different types of scholarships are available.
   B. There are many sports scholarship.
   C. It is hard to get a good scholarship.
   D. Academic scholarships are harder to get than sports scholarships.

Listen the teacher talking about essays in a writing class.

(Professor) Today, I want to talk about essays. Many writers find essays difficult to write, but some of our greatest writers have been essayists. They take their ideas and write their opinion on a subject and explain why it should be important to us.

E. B. White is a good example. White wrote an essay called "The Hen: An Appreciation." It was written in 1944 during the Second World War and is pretty famous. In his essay, he talks about such things as showing the hens respect, and "her elegance and girlish ways". Who talks about chickens that way? No one I know!

Essays were a pretty dull and unappreciated form of writing at first, but later, according to the Oxford Companion to the English Language, became "reflective, elegant, and philosophical". We can see all three qualities in White's essay. He is elegant in describing the attributes of the hens. He is philosophical when he discusses the difficulties he faced over long periods of time with his hens. He claims their relationship was "not easy to maintain". And finally, he is reflective throughout the piece. He says, "Chickens do not always enjoy an honorable position among city-bred people, although the egg, I notice, goes on and on."

I urge you to read the complete essay. It is a fine example of all the qualities expected in a good essay. Questions about will be on our next quiz, and you should be thoroughly familiar with it. Moving on.

9. How does the professor feel about studying White?

    A. He thinks it would be rewarding.
    B. He believes that it is useless.
    C. He says that it will be on the test.
    D. He believes studying essay writing is uninteresting.

10. The professor has all of the following reactions to the essay on hens EXCEPT

    A. He thinks it is humorous.
    B. He thinks it is an unusual subject.
    C. He believes it follows the rules of a good essay
    D. He believes the subject of the essay is inappropriate.

11. What does the professor say about early essays? *Choose 2 answers.*

    A. They were not valued.
    B. They were philosophical.
    C. They were exciting.
    D. They were unimaginative.

12. What is the lecture mainly about?

    A. The history of the essay
    B. E. B. White's contributions to the essay
    C. An analysis of White's essay on "The Hen"
    D. The essay

Reading Questions

Reading Comprehension
-50 questions about reading passages

Part 3

Reading Comprehension

Directions: Read the passage. Then answer the questions.

1	No one knows exactly how chocolate was discovered. Approximately, one thousand years ago, somewhere in Central America, the Mayan Indians began to roast the odd shaped fruit and use the seeds in a drink called *chocolatl* or *xocoatl*. This "bitter water" has evolved into what we know today as hot chocolate.
2	Historians believe that the way to use and enjoy the cocoa fruit was discovered over 2500 years ago. The fruit was probably used for the pulp which was slightly acidic. Later the beans or seeds were roasted and **pulverized** to make a thick, **coarse** paste. This paste was flavored with different seeds, vanilla, chilies and honey. After the paste was flavored, it was allowed to dry. The chocolate paste became hard and could easily be transported by the natives in rectangular shapes called tablets. The natives used the chocolate tablets to make a drink by dissolving the tablets in water and whipping it until frothy.
3	Columbus discovered chocolate on his fourth trip to the Americas. He did not like the drink as prepared by the natives. Yet, he realized the beans were valuable to the Mayans because they rushed to pick up some beans that fell when the Spaniards were loading their ship with **them**. He carried some beans back to King Ferdinand V of Spain who was not impressed with them at first.
4	Hernan Cortez discovered also the value of the cocoa beans when he found Moctezuma's treasury. He had expected to find gold, but instead he found more than one billion cocoa beans. The Spaniard realized they were valuable, but he wasn't sure exactly how.
5	Cortez learned how to prepare chocolate and carried his knowledge back to Spain where it remained unpopular. In 1530 and 1540, the nuns at the Guanaco convent in South America began adding sugar and vanilla to the drink. This made the drink more popular to the European palate.
6	For almost 100 years, Spain and her colonies maintained a **monopoly** on the cocoa beans. In 1606, the monopoly ended and other European nations began to obtain the cocoa beans and produce chocolate.
7	The cocoa beverage became very popular in Europe through the royal courts and the nobility. Chocolate houses were the rage, yet the drink would probably not appeal to us today. The drink was thick, acrid, and greasy.
8	Many attempts were made to eliminate the bitterness and oiliness by adding wheat, corn or oat flour. Nothing worked until Coenraad van Houten invented a hydraulic press that could extract two thirds of the fat. The press had two great advantages. It could eliminate most of the fat which could be used to make chocolate for eating, and it could use the remains of the paste for grinding into cocoa powder. The alkalizing process, called *dutching*, allowed the powder to remain suspended in liquids for longer periods of time.
9	The manufacture of modern chocolate candy began over 150 years ago in Sweden by the Swiss brothers Cloetta who built their Steam-Chocolate-Factory in the city of Malmo. When another Swiss discovered how to manufacture milk solids, the milk chocolate candy bar was

	created.
10	In modern times, chocolate **confections** became a billion dollar industry. The world's biggest consumer of chocolate is Switzerland with an average of 19.8 pounds per person followed by Germany at 17.4 pounds. The United States comes in ninth on this chart with only 9.5 pounds per person. According to Statista in 2016, worldwide chocolate confectionery consumption was a staggering 7.3 million tons in 2015-2016. Milk chocolate is the preferred flavor with over 50% of the market.
11	Even though cocoa beans were discovered in the Americas, more than two-thirds of the world's production comes from West Africa. The largest company in the world that manufactures and sells chocolate and cocoa products is Barry Callebaut. This wholesaler, a business-to-business (b2b) entity, produces chocolate that appears in one of five products around the world. About 42% and 26% of their chocolate products are sold to Europe and America respectively of an astonishing 1.8 million tonnes.
Sources	Young, A.M. The chocolate tree—a natural history of chocolate. Washington: Smithsonian Institute Press. Barry Callebaut website: https://www.barry-callebaut.com/at-a-glance

Directions: Answer the following questions.

1. The word "pulverized" in paragraph 2 is closest in meaning to

    A. carefully preserved
    B. decimated
    C. destroyed
    D. crushed

2. The word "coarse" in paragraph 2 is closest in meaning to

    A. rough
    B. consisting of large particles
    C. fine or delicate
    D. uneven

3. Which of the following made the tablets easy to transport?

    A. The tablets were hard and dry.
    B. The tablets were stackable.
    C. The tablets were small.
    D. The tablets were easily broken.

4. What can be inferred from paragraph 1 and 2 as reasons King Ferdinand V did not like the chocolate drink?

   A. The drink was not well prepared
   B. His friends did not like the drink either.
   C. The drink was bitter.
   D. The flavors were unusual.

5. What does the word them in paragraph 3 refer to?

   A. Beans
   B. Natives
   C. Mayans
   D. Ship

6. What can be inferred from paragraph 4 about Cortez's discovery of the cocoa beans?

   A. He was probably disappointed.
   B. He was excited.
   C. He was elated about the discovery.
   D. He was saddened.

7. Select the TWO answer choices that are mentioned in paragraph 5 as being reasons chocolate became popular in the 1500s. *To receive credit, you must select TWO answers.*

   A. The nuns flavor the chocolate drink with vanilla.
   B. The nuns made the drink more popular to Europeans.
   C. The European palate was more refined.
   D. The drink had added sugar.

8. The word 'monopoly' in paragraph 6 is closest in meaning to

   A. exclusive control
   B. right to sell in large quantities
   C. ability to exploit the market
   D. cartel

9. Select TWO answer choices mentioned in paragraph 8 as being reasons the hydraulic press improved the processing of chocolate. To receive credit, you must select TWO answers.

   A. It could eliminate most of the chocolate.
   B. It could eliminate most of the fat.
   C. It could use the remains of the paste.
   D. It could grind the beans into powder.

10. **In paragraph 8, there is a missing sentence. The paragraph is repeated below and show four letters (A, B, C, and D) that indicate where the following sentence could be added.**

Van Houten also discovered how to neutralize the acidity of the product by using potash.

Many attempts were made to eliminate the bitterness and oiliness by adding wheat, corn or oat flour. **(A)** Nothing worked until Coenraad van Houten invented a hydraulic press that could extract two thirds of the fat. The press had two great advantages. **(B)** It could eliminate most of the fat which could be used to make chocolate for eating, and it could use the remains of the paste for grinding into cocoa powder. **(C)** The alkalizing process, called *dutching*, allowed the powder to remain suspended in liquids for longer periods of time. **(D)**

   A. Option A
   B. Option B
   C. Option C
   D. Option D

11. The word 'confections' in paragraph 10 is closest in meaning to

   A. cakes
   B. candy
   C. desserts
   D. any type of sweet preparation

12. In paragraph 10, which one of the following is **NOT** mentioned as a major statistic about chocolate?

   A. Worldwide chocolate consumption was 7.3 million tons in 2015-2016.
   B. Milk chocolate accounted for over 50% of the total consumption.
   C. The Swiss eat the most chocolate.
   D. The United States prefers milk chocolate to other types of chocolate.

13. In paragraph 11, all of the following statements are mentioned EXCEPT

    A. 2/3 of the cocoa production comes from Central America.
    B. Barry Callehaut is the largest b2b chocolate company in the world.
    C. Callehaut sells about 42% of their products to Europe.
    D. Callehaut sells about 1.8 million tonnes to Europe and America annually.

14. Directions: An introductory sentence for a brief summary of the passage is provided below. Complete the summary by selecting the THREE answer choices that express the most important ideas in the passage. Some sentences do not belong in the summary because they express ideas that are not presented in the passage or are minor ideas in the passage. *This question is worth 2 points.*

Write your answer choices in the spaces where they belong. You can either write the letter of your answer choice or you can copy the sentence.

Chocolate has grown in popularity over the years, but at first, it was not popular in Europe.
•
•
•

A. Chocolate was first discovered in the Americas about 2500 years ago.
B. Columbus and King Ferdinand V did not like chocolate at first.
C. Because of nun in the Guanaco convent, chocolate became more popular.
D. Today, chocolate is a billion dollar industry.
E. The hydraulic press extracted 2/3 of the fat making modern chocolate possible.
F. Cortez had a more important role in the popularization of chocolate than Columbus.

	The African Violet
1	The history of the African violet is one where a species from Africa took the world by storm for many reasons. The violet was discovered in 1892 in the Usambara Mountains in Tanganyika (now Tanzania) by Baron Walter von Saint Paul. He sent seeds and maybe some plants to his father in Germany. The Director of the Royal Botanic Garden declared them a new **species**.
2	The plant was named *Saintpaulia ionantlia*. The *Saintpaulia* was to honor the discoverer of the plants. The Greek word ***ionantha*** means with violet like flowers. Many years later, another botanist discovered that there were actually two species in the plants sent to Germany by Baron von Saint Paul. This second species was named *Saintpaulia confusa*.
3	In 1893, the first African violets were shipped to a New York from Europe. Years later, the Armacost and Royston Nursery in Los Angeles obtained seeds from Germany and England. From their seedlings, the nursery selected ten plants became known as the original ten. These ten seedlings and two species plants have produced most of the over 18,000 registered plants in existence today through **hybridizing**.
4	Over the years, several more species plants were added to the original classification of the *Saintpaulia* and increased the known varieties to more than twenty. They were later reduced to six. However, modern DNA testing has entered the **fray** and in 2015, the species were listed as ten. Scientists studied their leaf structure, geographical location in the wild and their evolutionary development.
5	The work of scientists in classifying African violets might seem **frivolous** at first, but the plants are extremely valuable commercially. The information the scientific community gives commercial growers, who are constantly creating new hybrids, contributes to the violet's commercial success. In 2015, the potted flowering plants were valued at $714 million with California and Florida being the two biggest growers. While this figure is reflective of all flowering indoor plants, African violets were a major player in this market. Commercial growers like African violets because they can produce a flowering plant in five to six weeks and because of the huge variety of plants. The African violet is called "America's favorite houseplant" for a reason!
	Sources: Bartholomew, P. and AVSA. Growing to Show. Rev. 2008. Waterloo, Iowa. Pioneer graphics, 119 p.. Nishii, K. et al Streptocarpus redefined to include all Afro-Malagasy Gesneriaceae:... Taxon 64 (6) December 2015: 1243-1274. USAD. Floriculture Crops. 2015 Summary.

15. The word 'species' in paragraph 1 is closest in meaning to
    A. Plant
    B. A distinct kind
    C. Different color
    D. Flowering plant

16. Where does the word *ionantha* in paragraph 2 come from

    A. Greek
    B. Germany
    C. Africa
    D. Europe

17. How did the African violet get the name *Saintpaulia*?

    A. From the native African culture.
    B. From the Greek
    C. From the last name of the discoverer
    D. From the Tanganyika language

18. The word 'hybridizing' in paragraph 3 is closest in meaning to

    A. Crossbreeding
    B. Mixing
    C. Purifying
    D. Detoxifying

19. The word 'fray' in paragraph 4 is closest in meaning to

    A. Discussion
    B. Talks
    C. Conversation
    D. Brawl

20. According to paragraph 4, how did scientists determine the current number of species? *Choose 2 answers.*

    A. By studying taxonomy charts
    B. By studying the DNA of the plants
    C. By studying their geographical location in the wild
    D. By looking at plants and their characteristics

21. Why is the scientific classification of the *Saintpaulia* important?

    A. It is an important commercial product.
    B. There is a huge number of varieties.
    C. Scientific knowledge satisfies our curiosity.
    D. The plants are easy to grow.

22. Write the letter or the sentence of the THREE (3) best answer choices that express the most important ideas of the passage. **This question is worth 2 points.**

The African violet is America's favorite houseplant for many reasons.
•
•
•

Choose 3 answers from the following choices.
1. African violets have many different hybrids.
2. African violets are a huge commercial success.
3. African violets are easy to grow.
4. Commercial growers can produce a crop in 5-6 weeks.
5. There are many more species that originally thought.
6. Flowering indoor plants, including African violets, are a huge economic market.

Reading Comprehension
Questions about reading passages
Nos. 23-50

Part 3_b

Reading Comprehension

Directions: Read the passage. Then answer the questions that follow the passage.

	MOUNTAINS
1	Mountains are all around us on the surface of the Earth and in the ocean's depths. They are caused by different types of movement of the Earth. Many mountains exist on each of the continents, but what are mountains? Geologists classify land masses of higher than 1,000 feet as mountains, and mountain close together as chains or mountain ranges.
2	Mountains often **function** as the boundaries between different countries (like the Pyrenees that separate Spain and Portugal) or mountains can act as a protective barrier that protect countries from invading armies. Switzerland has used their natural landscape to prevent invasions and to provide refuge for centuries. Because of the high Alps, Switzerland has remained neutral for most of its existence.
3	There are four main types of mountains: fault-block mountains (such as the Sierra Nevada in California), volcanic mountains (such as Mount St. Helens in Washington State), dome mountains (such as the Black Hills of South Dakota), and plateau mountains (such as mountains in New Zealand).
4	Simply explained, plate tectonics cause gigantic pieces of the Earth's crust to fold and **buckle** or break into blocks. Volcanic and fault-block mountains form when the plates collide with each other. The crust (also called lithosphere) 'floats' on the surface of the Earth. Beneath the lithosphere lies the asthenosphere, a layer of solid rock that **is subjected to** so much heat and pressure that is becomes liquid. If the asthenosphere pushes through the cracks and rises, it causes fault-block mountains. If the crust breaks into gigantic blocks; the blocks can move up and down and may stack on top of each other.
5	**Dome** mountains are formed when the magma rises up but doesn't break through the surface of the Earth's crust. As the dome hardens, it remains higher than the surrounding area and is worn away by wind and rain erosion. The mountains become more circular and have rounded tops.
6	Plateau mountains are formed in a way similar to dome mountains. The tectonic plates push up huge chunks of land, but without folding or faulting. These mountains are then formed by other elements such as erosion or **weathering**.
7	Mountains impact our lives and play. They affect our weather, the flow of water, and animal and plant life. When mountains are formed by volcanic eruptions, minerals are brought to the surface. Because many rivers begin in the high mountain peaks, mountains are good place to build electric power stations. Mountains provide the **site** for many winter sports, such as skiing and snowboarding. Since man cannot move mountains, he has learned to live with nature's landscape.
SOURCES	Barrow, M. The Mountain Environment. http://www.primaryhomeworkhelp.co.uk/mountains/types.htm

	Mountains: highest points on Earth. http://science.nationalgeographic.com/science/earth/surface-of-the-earth/mountains-article

23. This passage is mainly about

    A. How mountains are made
    B. Description of the different types of mountains
    C. How mountains function
    D. Description of mountains and their functions

24. The word 'function' in paragraph 2 is closest in meaning to

    A. Act
    B. Goal
    C. Work
    D. Power

25. In paragraph 2, all of the following are given as reasons mountains protect humans EXCEPT

    A. To establish borders between countries
    B. To deter enemies
    C. To provide recreation
    D. To prevent invading armies

26. What can be inferred from the information in paragraphs 2 and 3 about mountains?

    A. Mountains are prevalent on Earth.
    B. Mountains are rare on the Earth's surface.
    C. Different types of mountains are formed in different locations on Earth.
    D. The Alps are domed mountains.

27. The word 'buckle' in paragraph 4 is closest in meaning to

    A. Yield
    B. Knuckle
    C. Bend
    D. Clasp

28. The words 'is subjected to' in paragraph 4 are closest in meaning to

   A. Is removed from
   B. Undergoes
   C. Is vulnerable to
   D. Experiences

29. What is plate tectonics?

   A. Blocks of Earth that move
   B. Movement of pieces of the Earth's crust
   C. Explanation of how mountains are formed
   D. Volcanoes that form mountains

30. Which of the following can be inferred from the description of plate tectonics in paragraph 4?

   A. Volcanic and fault-block mountains are formed in the same way.
   B. Any amount of force can cause a plate to collide with another plate
   C. Plates exist in only a few countries.
   D. The surface of the Earth is in constant motion.

31. The word 'dome' in paragraph 5 is closest in meaning to

   A. Cupola
   B. Oval
   C. Ragged
   D. peaked

32. The word 'weathering' in paragraph 6 is closest in meaning to

   A. effects of natural elements on a mountain
   B. physical effects on land surfaces
   C. chemical effects on mountains
   D. changed by rain

33. The word 'site' in paragraph 7 is closest in meaning to

    A. sitting room
    B. place
    C. resort
    D. land

34. In paragraph 7 of the passage, a sentence is missing. Look at the paragraph, which is repeated below, and choose one of the four letters (A, B, C, and D) to indicate where the following sentence could be added.

Because many rivers begin in the high mountain peaks, mountains are good place to build electric power stations.

Mountains impact our lives and play. They affect our weather, the flow of water, and animal and plant life. (A) When mountains are formed by volcanic eruptions, minerals are brought to the surface. (B) Mountains provide the **site** for many winter sports, such as skiing and snowboarding. (C) Since man cannot move mountains, he has learned to live with nature's landscape. (D)

    A. Option A
    B. Option B
    C. Option C
    D. Option D

35. **Directions: In the following table, a sentence is provided to introduce a summary of the passage. Choose THREE more sentences from the sentences below to complete your summary. Some of the sentences given are not included in the passage or are minor ideas from the passage.** *The question is worth 2 points.*

Write your answers in the space below. You can just write the letter of the sentence or copy the whole sentence.

Mountains are formed by powerful geological forces and mankind has learned how to use them to his advantage.
•
•
•

Answer Choices

A. Mountains have many functions in the development of different countries.

B. Plate tectonics can be used to explain how mountains are formed.

C. Dome mountains are formed by magma.

D. Weathering shapes plateau mountains.

E. Mountains determine how we work and many of our sports.

F. Natural forces shape the Earth.

Directions: Read the passage. Then answer the questions that follow the passage.

1	Positive psychology is a relatively new branch of psychology. It can be defined as the scientific study of happiness or as the study of the strengths that enable people and communities to succeed. Positive psychology tries to explain and understand happiness and well-being. Throughout history, mankind has looked for explanations for these human **traits.** Socrates said, "The secret of change is to focus all of your energy, not on fighting the old, but on building the new." He believed in knowing oneself.
2	Despite the long history of happiness, psychologists dwelt on digging into people's pasts, **ferreting out** their secrets, and analyzing minute details of their pasts. Positive psychology is just the opposite. It emphasizes the importance building on the positive aspects of people's lives and helping them enjoy their present and having hope for a happy future.
3	Positive psychology was first proposed in 1998 by Martin Seligman, a University of Pennsylvania psychologist. In his address to the American Psychological Association, he started a new movement in psychology by **exhorting** his fellow psychologists to "turn toward understanding and building the human strengths to complement our emphasis on healing damage." In his book *Flourish: A Visionary New Understanding of Happiness and Well-being (2011)*, Seligman expanded his theory to include positive relationships and accomplishments.
4	Positive psychology has since focused on three areas of human **endeavor**: positive emotions, positive individual traits and positive institutions. To develop positive emotions, people must be content with their past, happy in the present and hopeful for the future. The individual's positive traits come from his or her individual strengths and virtues. Positive institutions focus on how to improve a community by utilizing its strengths.
5	We don't need to be happy or joyful all the time. Happiness is not a response to dangerous situations. We need a range of emotions to help protect us from dangerous—fight or flight—situations. We need happiness and joy to compensate for the negative emotions in order to live a positive life as we **seek** happiness. Joy is the ultimate response that we can experience, but we can't sustain it for long. Joy is **fleeting**.
6	Another key to positive change is positive relationships. Married couples are happier than single people. Researchers debate the reasons why, but the fact remains that happily married couples live longer, have better social skills, and are healthier.
7	Strong and healthy social ties are another key to positive living. The Framingham Heart Study found that happiness and unhappiness tended to spread through close relationships. Researchers found that happiness spread more consistently than unhappiness through the network. Having a good friend helps people **cushion** the impact of negative life experiences, and thus, increases one's self-esteem. Social interactions, such as a gift of flowers, may affect a wide variety of emotions.
8	Age does matter. Researchers have shown that during their 20s and 70s, individuals are happier than during the decades of the 40s and 50s. The reasons are not entirely clear, but some facts stand out. After the 20s, feelings of stress and anger decline. Perhaps it is because certain social skills take time to develop or perhaps it is because hormones become more stabilized. Older people have more health problems, but fewer problems in general.
9	Money cannot buy happiness according to the old **saying**. Research seems to support this

	adage. Money is important to the poor who have not met their basic needs, but less so to the middle class and the wealthy. Lottery winners have higher levels of happiness immediately after winning, but the happiness level soon drops and returns to previous levels within a short period of time.
10	Personality plays an important part in our happiness. **Genetics** play a role in our personality and the emotions associated with personality. Neuroscientists believe that genetics control approximately 80% of our long-term sense of well-being leaving 20% that can be influenced by the environment and learning from sources such as positive change.
11	Many researchers believe that individual differences are important, but research to date suggests that most people will benefit from the **doctrines** of Positive Psychology. Psychologists will continue to develop new techniques and exercises to improve our daily lives, and this is good. All human experience moves forward by experimenting, discarding the things that don't work well and accepting new challenges.

36. What is the main idea of the passage?

   A. Positive Psychology is good for us.
   B. Positive Psychology is a new field.
   C. What is Positive Psychology?
   D. An explanation of Seligman's theory.

37. The word 'traits' in paragraph 1 is closest in meaning to

   A. Quantity
   B. Individual
   C. Quality
   D. Ideology

38. The words 'ferreting out' in paragraph 2 is closest in meaning to

   A. secreting
   B. searching for
   C. disguising
   D. suppressing

39. The word 'exhorted' in paragraph 3 is closest in meaning to

    A. Impeded
    B. Absolved
    C. Deterred
    D. Urged

40. All of the following are mentioned in paragraph 4 as elements of Positive Psychology EXCEPT

    A. Positive emotions
    B. Positive institutions
    C. Positive communities
    D. Positive individual traits

41. The word 'fleeting' in paragraph 5 is closest in meaning to

    A. Short-lived
    B. Persistent
    C. Lasting
    D. Enduring

42. The word 'cushion' in paragraph 7 is closest in meaning to

    A. Harden
    B. An object to sit on
    C. Absorb
    D. Encircle

43. Which of the following is NOT mentioned in paragraph 7 as a reason that social ties are important?

    A. Good friends lessen the impact of negative life experiences.
    B. Good friends increase a person's self-esteem.
    C. Social interactions may affect a wide variety of emotions.
    D. Happiness is easier to spread than unhappiness in social networks.

44. All of the following are mentioned in paragraph 8 as reasons why age matters in happiness EXCEPT

    A. Hormones settle down after the 20s.
    B. Older people have fewer problems in general.
    C. Older people don't have problems getting around.
    D. Stress and anger decline in the 20s.

45. The word 'saying' in paragraph 9 is closest in meaning to

    A. Talking
    B. Sawyer
    C. Spreading
    D. Proverb

46. What can be inferred from paragraph 9 about money and happiness?

    A. Money can't buy happiness.
    B. The poor are happier.
    C. The middle class have their basic needs met.
    D. The wealthy are very happy.

47. The word 'genetics' in paragraph 10 is closest in meaning to

    A. Branch of biology
    B. Study of history
    C. Family
    D. Relatives

48. The word 'doctrines' in paragraph 11 is closest in meaning to

    A. Evidence
    B. Documentation
    C. Stubborn
    D. Dogmas

49. In paragraph 10, a sentence has been left out. The paragraph is repeated below and shows four letters (A, B, C, D) that indicate where the sentence below could be added.

Extroverts seem to be happier and perhaps this is because they develop stronger relationships and have more support groups than introverts.

(A) Personality plays an important part in our happiness. **(B)** <u>Genetics</u> play a role in our personality and the emotions associated with personality. **(C)** Neuroscientists believe that genetics control approximately 80% of our long-term sense of well-being leaving 20% that can be influenced by the environment and learning from sources such as positive change. **(D)**

- A. Option A
- B. Option B
- C. Option C
- D. Option D

50. Directions: An beginning sentence for a short summary of the passage is given below. Complete the summary by choosing THREE answer choices that express the most important ideas in the passage. Some of the sentences may present ideas not presented in the passage or are minor details. *This question is worth 2 points.*

You may write the letter of your choice or you can copy your sentence in the spaces below.

Positive Psychology is a new branch of psychology.
•
•
•

Answer Choices

A. According to Positive Psychology, we can determine our own happiness.

B. Positive Psychology has focused on three areas of human endeavor.

C. Positive Psychology was the brain-child of an unknown psychologist.

D. We don't have to be happy all the time.

E. Factors, such as health, wealth, and social status, are important in our happiness level.

F. Money, age, and personality are factors that are an important part of our happiness.

Structure & Expression Questions

Structure and Written Expression
-15 exercises of completing sentences correctly
-25 exercises of identifying errors

Structure and Written Expression

Part 1

Complete the following sentences.

1. None of the food _____ fresh.

A. tastes
B. were
C. tasting
D. taste

2. I have seen _____ interesting movies recently.

A. some
B. the
C. any
D. an

3. I congratulated the manager _____ his new promotion.

A. for
B. by
C. at
D. on

4. You're studying chemistry, _____ you?

A. are
B. was
C. aren't
D. do

5. Jane has a bad cold. She _____ better see a doctor.

A. should
B. had
C. ought
D. ought to

6. The Mississippi river is a waterway _____ is used to carry boats with goods and passengers.

A. who
B. whom
C. which
D. that

7. Yesterday, I went to the movies. I had a soda and a hot dog. I still wanted _____ ice cream when we got out.

A. some
B. no
C. any
D. few

8. I get my exercise by running, cycling, and _____.

A. swimming
B. to play soccer
C. I have taken classes of tennis
D. being a boxer

9. Our coach gave us _____ because we couldn't settle down after we lost the football game.

A. some criticism
B. a hard time
C. a shout
D. a thing or two

10. The study on cancer is showing how new technologies are improving cancer treatments. _____ a major study conducted by the Mayo Clinic.

A. Its
B. Its'
C. Its is
D. It's

11. If you meet me by four, we _____ to the movies at five.

A. go
B. will go
C. went
D. have gone

12. I _____ the football stadium from my balcony.

A. will see
B. can see
C. might see
D. had seen

13. Hamlet _____ by Shakespeare.

A. had been written
B. has been written
C. was written
D. is written

14. _____ you paid for the tickets to the movie, I will pay for the sodas and popcorn.

A. Now that
B. Because of
C. But
D. Since

15. I had promised my mom _____ my room after I took my shower.

A. cleaning
B. to look at
C. to clean up
D. washing

Part 2

Directions: In this section of the test, you will read a series of short texts created by nonnative English speakers. You will be asked to identify the errors in the students' writing.

Questions 1 – 3 are based on the following text about a popular sport in the student's native country.

Cycling of the world is a very popular sport in every country. Cyclists must has the skill to ride a bicycle without stopping for many miles. They train every day so that he can become world class racers.

1. In the first sentence, the error is in the relative order of:

A. A noun and an adjective
B. The direct and indirect object
C. The subject and object
D. The prepositional phrases

2. In sentence two, there is an error in:

A. Agreement between noun and verb
B. Pronoun and antecedent
C. Structure of the subordinate clause
D. Order of the sentence elements

3. In the last sentence, there is an error in the:

A. Noun and an adjective
B. Direct and indirect objects
C. Subject and the object
D. Pronoun form

Questions 4-6 are based on an excerpt from an essay describing the student's favorite foods.

My favorite food for breakfast is a bread and a cheese with a cup of coffee and milk. In my country we eat a lot of beef. There is always any kind of rice at every meal, too. For snacks, we eat meat pastries called empanadas. Tourists in my country likes to eat fruit or a small square of guava paste for dessert.

4. In the first sentence, there is an error in the:

A. Verb tense
B. Parallel structure
C. Punctuation
D. Subject and object

5. In sentence number three, the word any is incorrect because:

A. Some is used with count nouns
B. Any is used with noncount nouns
C. Any is used in questions
D. Any is used in negative statements

6. In the last sentence, the correct form of the verb likes should be:

A. like
B. liked
C. will like
D. have liked

Answer the questions following each text.

7. I am studying Computer Science. I have the second semester.
The verb was in the second sentence is incorrect with respect to:

A. Tense
B. Gender
C. Person
D. Number

8. I love my boyfriend too much.
The adverb too is incorrect with regards to:

A. Word order
B. Form
C. Spelling
D. Usage

9. My baby sister causes much problems every day.
 The word much is incorrect because:

A. It is used with countable nouns.
B. It is used with no count nouns.
C. It is used with collective nouns.
D. It is used with compound nouns.

10. The football game started on time, but we were late getting their.
The word their is incorrect because:

A. Their is a possessive adjective used to indicate place.
B. Their is singular and should be plural.
C. Their is a preposition.
D. Their is a personal pronoun.

11. The beer in these glasses are bitter.
The word are is incorrect because:

A. The verb are is correct
B. The verb are should come after the subject beer.
C. The verb are is incorrect because the subject is beer.
D. The verb are is in the present tense and should be in the past.

In the following section, there may be an error in grammar, usage, word choice, or idioms. Parts of the sentence may be underlined. All other parts of the sentence are correct. Select the underlined word or words that are incorrect. Mark the incorrect answer on your answer sheet.

12. My favorite teacher is the only person who is completely qualified to teach English literature to high school.
                                A   B   C   D

13. When the new Congress took office, legislation that had been ignored for years is urgent.
     A   B   C   D

14. The coup in Turkey failed when the government overcome the rebellious military.
      A   B   C   D

15. Neither snow or hail will keep postmen from their appointed rounds.
              A   B   C   D

16. Some people prefer vanilla, others prefer chocolate. I prefer the later.
            A   B C   D

17. She worked during the summer not because she was needing the money, but because she wanted the experience.
               A   B   C   D

18. The accident occurred <u>when</u> the school <u>bus,</u> carrying<u> students</u> overturned <u>on</u> the highway.
                                 A   B   C   D

19. The crowds <u>wandered</u> along the streets slowly <u>taking in</u> the sight of vendors selling <u>they're</u> <u>wares</u>.
                   A   B   C   D

20. The weather has been <u>very</u> hot. <u>However</u>, we have had three <u>weeks</u> of temperatures over 90
                         A   B   C

<u>degrees</u> Fahrenheit.
D

21. I enjoy visiting my grandmother on her birthday. <u>Some</u> of my <u>relatives</u> have returned <u>back</u> every year
                                              A   B   C

for the <u>last</u> twenty-five years.
       D

22. Exercise is a way to <u>improving</u> <u>your</u> <u>health,</u> especially if you do <u>it</u> often.
                   A   B   C   D

23. John and I went <u>walking</u> on Saturday. <u>After</u> a few <u>blocks</u>, I ask him why he was walking so <u>slow</u>.
                  A   B   C   D

24. The manager <u>offered</u> me a <u>fair</u> salary compared to his <u>assistant's</u>, but not as much <u>like</u> I wanted.
               A   B   C   D

25. <u>Even though</u> times are tough, <u>both</u> of the banks <u>gives</u> loans to <u>qualified</u> students.
     A   B   C   D

Writing Essay Question

Writing

One essay question with 250-300 words in average

Reading passage

Political campaigns in the United States have an interesting history. At first, the candidates for president were decided by caucuses of the parties' congressional delegates. This didn't work too well because there were many abuses by party leaders. The primary elections tried to eliminate the problems of corruption.

In the primary elections, each party establishes its own rules in each state. In the beginning, each party—Republican and Democratic—gave each state two votes based on the number of electors they had in the Electoral College. (The number of members of the Electoral College has changed over time as new states were added to the United States. Currently, there are 538 votes.) The number of delegates for both parties has changed considerably over the years. In the 2016 elections, the Republican Party had 2,472 delegates, and the Democrats had 1,151. It can be complicated because each party makes its own rules about how many delegates each state will have. Some states give all of the delegates to the winner, but other states award the delegate proportionally.

Directions: Here is the transcript of a lecture.

Narrator: Now listen to part of a lecture on the topic you just read about.

Professor: Many people like to go to the national conventions. There is a lot of pageantry and high drama that goes on during the convention. The main purpose of the national political conventions is to select the person that will be the party's candidate in the presidential election. Many years ago, the political conventions were more important than they are today.

Why, do you ask, are the conventions less important? Well, because the primaries and the caucuses pretty much decide who will be nominated before the conventions begin. The conventions official role is to formally elect the candidate who will represent the party.

Some people believe that the enthusiasm shown at the nation conventions is important in getting people out to vote. Others say that party unity is strengthened in national conventions. Me, I don't know if this is necessary any more. The Internet and social media may replace the physical convention just as they have in other places in our lives.

Anyway, for now, we have national conventions that are huge, comical and fiercely debated. It is a stage for the candidate to be introduced formally to the electorate. It is also an opportunity for the party to introduce their platform. This is not a platform like an oil drilling platform, but rather a platform that is the party's stand on different issues and its principles.

Directions: You will have 20 minutes to prepare and write your response. The essay will be evaluated on how well you summarize the main points in the lecture and their connect with the reading text. Your response should be between 150 – 225 words long. You can consult the text while preparing your answer.

Summarize the main points made in the professor's talk, and explain how they contrast to the reading.

Listening Answers

LISTENING

Directions: The listening section evaluates your capacity to understand conversations and lectures in English. In this section, you will hear several short conversations and answer questions about these conversations. The questions frequently ask about the main idea and supporting details. Sometimes the questions ask about the speaker's purpose or attitude. Always answer the questions using what is said or implied by the speakers.

Most questions are worth one point. If the question is worth more, it will be stated in the directions.

During the actual test, you will be able to take notes and use the notes to answer the questions. Your notes will not be evaluated.

Part 1

(Female speaker) I recently studied a paper on morphology for my teacher's certificate. Morphology is so hard. My teacher was really great though. He made morphology interesting and tied it to different languages. Even so, I didn't understand a lot of the class and I hated it.

1. What did the woman say made the class easier to understand?

   A. The professor
   B. The paper was easy to understand
   C. Her teaching background
   D. Her ability to understand other languages

ANSWER: A. The professor
The woman says morphology is hard to understand so we can infer that the paper was difficult to understand. Her teaching background did not help because she had difficulty understanding the subject. The teacher ties the material to other languages, but the text does not state that the woman understood other languages. The correct answer is A. The professor.

2. Which sentence best expresses what the woman means when she says:
   He made morphology interesting and <u>tied it</u> to different languages.

   A. fixed it to other morphologies
   B. connected it to other languages
   C. explained it in the student's native language
   D. explained morphology in terms the woman could understand

Answer: B. connected it to other languages

The correct option is B. because the teacher tried to connect English morphology to other languages so the students could understand that morphology can be universal.

(Male student) Last night I watched the soccer match between Portugal and France. Everyone expected France to win, but Portugal won in the last seconds of the game. What a surprise! I have never seen a game I enjoyed more.

3. What was the man doing last night?

   A. Enjoying a football game
   B. Watching an exciting soccer game
   C. Watching his favorite team
   D. Enjoying a relaxing soccer game

ANSWER: B. Watching an exciting soccer game
In the United States, the term football is used to refer to American football, a contact sport played with an oval ball. The man watched the soccer match between two teams, but the text never states what his favorite team is. The soccer game was exciting because Portugal won in the last seconds of the game so it wasn't relaxing. The correct choice is B.

(Male student) Tomorrow I am going to the soccer stadium to watch our team defeat their opponents. I know we will win because we have the best team. Even though, we have several injuries, three of our players are going to the Olympics, and one of the players won the best player award last year.

4. Why does the man believe that his team is the best *team? Choose 2 answers.*

   A. Three players are going to the Olympics
   B. Their keeper has the fewest goals scored against him
   C. Several of their players are injured.
   D. Last year, one of their players was the best player.

Answers: A. Three players are going to the Olympics AND D. Last year, one of their players was the best player.
The two best answers are A and D. Injured players will not be able to play in the game. The keeper's saves and missed balls are not mentioned.

(Male student) I have backpacked around Europe before and never had any problems. Traveling by yourself forces you to try to communicate with the local people. It's a great way to meet people you wouldn't if you were traveling with friends. I like to carry a small notebook with me to write my observations in when I was eating alone in a small café or restaurant. Most of the time, I would talk to other diners and forget my notebook. Traveling alone is great because you can do whatever you want to and you don't have to do what the group is doing. There are two big drawbacks however. One is it can be more expensive. It's cheaper when you share a room with a friend. Sometimes, it gets lonely. Still, I think you should try it.

5. What is the main idea of the paragraph?

A. The man recommends traveling in a group.
B. The man likes to travel alone.
C. The man feels that traveling alone is more expensive.
D. The man thinks traveling with a small group of friends is better.

Answer: B. The man likes to travel alone.
The man likes to travel alone and gives several reasons for it.

6. According to the man, what all of the following are reasons to travel alone EXCEPT.

A. Sometimes, it gets lonely if you travel by yourself.
B. You can do whatever the group wants to do.
C. It is cheaper when you share a room.
D. You meet more people.

Answer: B. You can do whatever the group wants to do.
The man gives Options A, C, and D as reasons to travel alone. B is the only exception.

(Female student) People forget their cell phones and wash them. I have had this happen to two different friends. One dropped her cell phone in the washing machine by accident. The other one didn't know her cell phone was in the back pocket of her jeans. They both tried to dry the phones out by using rice, but they were not successful. I thought these stories were so funny, but they were really expensive mistakes.

7. Why did the people wash their cell phones?

    A. It was a class assignment.
    B. They were experimenting.
    C. They were funny jokes.
    D. They were expensive mistakes.

Answer: D. They were expensive mistakes.
The woman says the stories were so funny, but really expensive mistake.

8. Why did the women put their phones in rice?

    A. They wanted to cook the rice.
    B. They believed the rice would dry the phones out.
    C. They thought that the rice would make the phones work again.
    D. They wanted the rice to neutralize the soap in the phone.

Answer: B. They believed the rice would dry the phones out.
The only answer mentioned in the text is B.

(Female student) My professor recently began using podcasts for our classes. She believes that her students like the newer technologies so much that they pay more attention to the podcasts than the textbook. Her philosophy is "If you can't lick them, join them".

I really like the idea of podcasts, but I don't know if I am going to like them if we have to study using them.

9. What does the woman's professor mean when she says "if you can't lick them, join them"?

    A. The professor means that you can't win if you continue to do the same things the same way.
    B. The professor means that you should try something new.
    C. The professor means that you must join others if they won't join you.
    D. The professor means that it is better to do what the students want to do.

Answer: C. The professor means that you must join others if they won't join you.

This idiom means if you can't stop someone from doing something, then do the same thing they are doing.

10. What can we infer is the reason the woman is uncertain she will like podcasts as part of her classes?

    A. The woman probably believes that the podcasts will be boring.
    B. The woman likes podcasts now, but she is afraid that they will be uninteresting later on.
    C. The woman believes that podcasts should be for her personal use, not study time.
    D. The professor has required her students to watch lots of podcasts.

Answer: C. The woman believes that podcasts should be for her personal use, not study time. The best choice is C because it is the answer that expresses the woman's uncertainty about the class podcasts.

(Female Student) Last weekend, I overheard my little sister talking on her cell phone with her best friend. She was telling her friend not to say anything to my mother about her grades in school. I think my sister is getting a bad grade in history or algebra. Those are her worst two subjects. My mother gets very upset when we don't get good grades. If I tell my mother, my sister may tell on me another time.

11. Why is the woman upset that she overheard the conversation?

    A. She is afraid that her friend will tell her mother something bad about her.
    B. She is worried about her little sister's chemistry grades.
    C. She believes that her sister may be getting bad grades in school.
    D. She feels like she has to keep the secret about the bad grades in history also.

Answer: C. She believes that her sister may be getting bad grades in school.
The woman is worried her sister's grades. She thinks they are probably in history or algebra because these are her sister's worst two subjects. The text doesn't mention chemistry. She doesn't say that the friend will talk to the woman's mother. She doesn't feel like she has to keep the secret about the bad grades in history because she doesn't know if it was history or algebra. It is only a supposition not a fact. Therefore, the correct answer is C.

12. Why is the woman worried about her mother's reaction?

    A. Because her mother doesn't like for the girls to get bad grades.
    B. Because her mother wants the girls to get home earlier.
    C. Because her mother will say they must study more.
    D. Because her mother punish them.

Answer: A. Because her mother doesn't like for the girls to get bad grades.
The woman only says her mother doesn't like it when the girls receive poor grades, but she doesn't talk about the consequences, such as getting home earlier, studying more, or being punished. Thus, A is the correct choice.

(Female speaker) One time when I was babysitting, I started getting cold, so I turned up the heat. I still didn't get warm, so I turned it up some more. I remember when the parents came in; they thought it was really hot in the house. I guess I was still cold, because I was so still.

13. Why does the woman turn up the heat the second time?

    A. She was hot.
    B. She was feverish.
    C. She was still cold.
    D. She was ill.

Answer: C. She was still cold.
Despite trying to get warm, the woman continued to be cold. She was not feverish or ill, but she was motionless. C is the best option.

14. Why was the woman still cold?

    A. She was not moving.
    B. She was getting sick.
    C. The house was cold.
    D. The parents were cold, too.

Answer: A. She was not moving.
These two questions demonstrate the different uses of the word still. In this case, the woman was not moving, and she became cold. A is the best option.

(Male student) I am just learning to use my smart phone as a GPS device. I have had some funny experiences. One time, I put in the address wrong. I typed in the number for one address, but the street name for another. Instead of going to my dentist's new office, I wound up at a house being demolished. I guess I'll have to be more careful in the future.

15. According to the man, what advice does he give about using GPS devices?

    A. He thinks these devices are a waste of time.
    B. He believes that they are great for most people.
    C. He believes if you aren't careful, you could have problems.
    D. He suggests using them only when you need them.

Answer: C. He believes you must be sure to type in the correct address.
The man is talking about being careful to type in the correct address. If you don't, you will not arrive at your destination like he did.

16. Why did the man go to a house being demolished?

    A. He didn't know how to use his phone.
    B. He was unfamiliar with GPS devices.
    C. He put in the wrong address.
    D. He was looking for a new address.

Answer: C. He put in the wrong address.
By typing in the number for one address, and the street name for different one, the man put in the wrong address. C is the correct option.

(Male student) Our teacher was explaining about different sleeping habits of people. Many people like to get up early and feel really good in the morning, but not me. I am a night owl. I don't really get going until about 6 P.M. She told us that a lot of people prefer to take power naps. She is a morning person, but she takes power naps, too. If I took a power nap, I would be so grouchy that no one could stand me!

17. What is the text mainly about?

    A. The man's sleep habits.
    B. The teachers sleeping habits.
    C. Different sleeping habits of people.
    D. The way we adjust to sleep.

Answer: C. Different sleeping habits of people.
Even though the sleeping habits of the man and the teacher are mentioned, the text is mainly about different sleeping habits of people in general.

18. What can we infer that "power naps" means?
    A. A short period of sleep
    B. A rejuvenating period of sleep
    C. A long sleep before bedtime
    D. A short, refreshing period of sleep

Answer: D. a short, refreshing period of sleep
The text refers to naps several times. We can infer that they are short periods of sleep. When we think of 'power' we can infer that the nap gives us strength to continue working, studying, or whatever we are doing.

19. What does the man mean when he says "I would be so <u>grouchy</u> that no one could stand me?"

    A. that he would be happy.
    B. That he would be cross.
    C. That he would be sleepy.
    D. That he would be wide awake.

Answer: B. That he would be cross.
The word 'grouchy' means "cross, peevish, irritable, or cranky".

(Male student) I am studying to be a doctor. My parents have always wanted me to be one. I like science, and I like to help people. We are just beginning to interact with patients, and I am really good at listening to them, but you know what? I would really like to be a chef. Boy it would really upset my parents if I gave up medical school to cook in our restaurant.

20. What does the man say he would like to be?

   A. A patient
   B. A chef
   C. A doctor
   D. A scientist

Answer: B. A chef
The man is studying to be a doctor, but he would really like to be a chef.

21. What can we infer his parents do?

   A. They work in their restaurant.
   B. They are doctors.
   C. They work in medicine.
   D. They are teachers.

Answer: A. They work in their restaurant.
The text only mentions the parents as wanting their son to be a doctor and having a restaurant. Thus, we can assume they work in a restaurant and want their son to do better. A is the best option.

22. Why does the man believe he is good with patients?

   A. He likes science.
   B. He likes to talk with people.
   C. He is a good listener.
   D. He gets good grades in med school.

Answer: C. He is good at listening.
The man has many good attributes, but he is just beginning to interact with patients. He says he is good at listening to them.

(Female student) My mom went to a convention in Albuquerque last week. She loved all the activities at the convention, but she was not well while she was there. First of all, she had to go up and down stairs a lot for the different presentations, so her knees hurt. Secondly, she had difficulty breathing. Since she is usually very healthy, she thought it was because of the high altitude.

(Male student) I know. In Mexico City, where I am from, is over 7,000 feet high. Sometimes, tourists get altitude sickness. It usually passes in a few days, but at first, it can be difficult to breathe.

23. Why did the woman's mother have difficulty breathing?

    A. Because Mexico City was very high.
    B. Because Albuquerque has a high altitude.
    C. Because she had to go downstairs for presentations.
    D. Because she has health problems.

Answer: B. Because Albuquerque has a high altitude.
The woman said her mother thought it was because of the high altitude in Albuquerque. She was not in Mexico City nor does she have health problems. She had to go up and down stairs, not just down.

24. When tourists get altitude sickness, all of the following happen EXCEPT

    A. It usually lasts several days.
    B. It causes breathing problems.
    C. They feel a little sick.
    D. They love all the activities.

Answer: D. They love all the activities.
The tourists have breathing problems and feel a little sick for a few days. The text says the woman's mother enjoyed all the activities at the convention, not the tourists in Mexico City.

25. Why did the woman's mother have problems with the presentations?

    A. She had to listen really well.
    B. She had difficulty hearing the speakers.
    C. She had problems with her headphones.
    D. She had to go up and down stairs.

Answer: D. She had to go up and down stairs.
The text states that the woman's mom's knees hurt because she had to go up and down stairs to get to the presentations. None of the other options are mentioned.

(Female student) Yesterday, I visited my grandma. I can't believe how old-fashioned she is. She didn't like my pink hair. I explained it was a fashion statement, not a true color. And then, she hated my tattoos. I only have three small tattoos: a dolphin on the back of my neck, a heart on my ankle and a butterfly on my wrist. She said that I would be sorry I had colored my skin with permanent ink because fashion comes and goes. Lucky for me, I had removed my nose ring, or she would have really been upset.

26. Why was the grandmother upset with her granddaughter?

    A. Because she didn't like the haircut.
    B. Because she didn't like tattoos the granddaughter chose.
    C. Because she had too many tattoos.
    D. Because the tattoos were permanent.

Answer: D. Because the tattoos were permanent.
The only reason given in the text was that the tattoos were permanent. No other reason is given for the grandmother's disapproval.

27. Why does the woman imply that her grandmother is old-fashioned?

    A. Because she doesn't like unusual hair colors.
    B. Because she the tattoos are of unpleasant objects.
    C. Because the grandmother didn't like her granddaughter's fashions.
    D. Because the grandmother has pink hair and tattoos on her ankle.

Answer: C. Because the grandmother didn't like her granddaughter's choices.

The granddaughter and the grandmother obviously have different opinions about modern day choices in hair color and the use of body art. Since, the grandmother didn't like the woman's hair color or her tattoos; we can infer that she is old-fashioned, at least according to her granddaughter, the woman.

(Female student) I have decided to become a vegetarian. I am not going to eat meat anymore. I really enjoy rice, beans, vegetables, and fruits, so why should I continue to eat meat? Sometimes, I get ill if I eat meat or chicken. I believe that animals deserve to live, too. I may become a vegan later on, but right now, I plan to still eat eggs and cheese. They are two of my favorite foods. And you can make a quiche with them.

28. Why is the woman becoming a vegetarian?

    A. Because she likes eggs and cheese.
    B. Because she likes vegetables.
    C. Because she doesn't like meat.
    D. Because of her health.

Answer: D. Because of her health.
The woman doesn't explain why, but she says that meat and chicken make her sick sometimes.

29. According to the text, what foods do vegetarians eat that vegans don't eat?

    A. Rice and beans
    B. Vegetables and fruits
    C. Cheese and eggs
    D. Fruits

Answer: C. Cheese and eggs
The text only mentions cheese and eggs though there may be many more factors determining the difference in the two lifestyles, but this is the only one mentioned in the text.

30. What are the woman's two favorite foods?

    A. Fruits and vegetables
    B. Vegetables and eggs
    C. Cheese and rice
    D. Cheese and eggs

Answer: D. Cheese and eggs

The woman says that she enjoys rice, beans, vegetables and fruits, but she two of her favorite foods are cheese and eggs.

LISTENING

Part 2

(CONVERSATION TRANSCRIPT)

(NARRATOR) Listen to a conversation between a female student and a male student and then answer the questions.

(Female student) Hi, James. Did you see the soccer game on TV yesterday?

(Male student) No. I had a lot of studying to do for the finals in chemistry. I prefer bicycle riding to soccer anyway.

(Female student) You do? I thought everyone liked soccer.

(Male student) I like soccer and basketball, but I prefer riding bicycles. What did you do over the weekend?

(Female student) Well, I had to work. My new boss is really demanding. She wants us all to know all the items on the menu and to keep the restaurant spotless.

(Male student) That's really great. You are getting good experience in the restaurant business.

(Female student) I know. The problem is when we are very busy; it's hard to remember everything. I started last summer so I know the menu pretty well, but it is hard with so many changes at once.

(Male student) What's your favorite food?

(Female student) Me? I like everything. I love tacos, spaghetti, pizza, and fried chicken. That's Mexican, Italian, and United States food. What a mixture.

(Male student) Wow, it's like the United States population. The people come here from so many different places. I guess they bring their favorite foods with them.

(Female student) I know. My parents came from Colombia. Their favorite food is beans and rice. They love to fry ripe plantains to go with them, and I love the flan they serve for dessert.

(Male student) Plantains? What are these things? What is flan?

(Female student giggling) Well, plantains are large bananas that must be cooked before you eat them. Flan is a baked custard or pudding made with eggs and milk. My mom makes it with caramel syrup. She turns it upside-down and cools it in the refrigerator for several hours or overnight. It is heaven in your mouth. So cold and creamy.

(Male student) Sounds good. Hey. Have you heard about the highways being widened in front of the university? That is going to cause so many problems for us coming to school.

(Female student) Why?

(Male student) Because the exits will be narrower and fewer during construction. It will be impossible to get to school quickly. We will have to get up earlier and leave home earlier.

(Female student) Not me. I walk to school, remember?

(Male student) Oh, yeah. I forgot. I've got to go. My test starts on the dot at 10.

(Female student) Hey, you better get going. It's a quarter until 10 right now.

1. What are the speakers mainly discussing?

A. How the woman should prepare for her class.
B. The woman's responsibilities at home.
C. The plans to widen the highway near the school.
D. Different events of everyday life.

ANSWER: D. Different events of everyday life.

Options A and B were not mentioned in the conversation. Option C was mentioned by the male speaker as an event happening in the future. Option D is the correct choice since both speakers talk about things that happened in their daily lives.

2. Who is difficult for the female speaker to please?

A. The male speaker
B. Her boss
C. Her parents
D. Her mom

ANSWER: B. Her boss.

The only person mentioned that gave the female speaker any problems was her boss.

3. There are two answers for the next question. *Mark the two answers.*

Why does the male speaker believe that the widening of the highway will cause difficulties for him to get to school?

A. The roads will be narrower.
B. There will be more traffic.
C. There will be many bicycles on the roads.
D. There will be fewer exits.

ANSWER: A. The roads will be narrower and D. There will be fewer exits.

The text does not mention that there will be more traffic or that there will be more bicycles on the roads.

4. Read part of the conversation again. Then answer the question.

    (Male student) Oh, yeah. I forgot. I've got to go. My test starts on the dot at 10.

    What does the man mean when he says: 'on the dot at 10?

A. The test begins around 10.
B. The test begins precisely at 10.
C. The test will start as soon as the students arrive for their 10 class.
D. The test at approximately 10 o'clock.

ANSWER: B. The test begins precisely at 10.

The expression 'on the dot at 10' means exactly or precisely at 10 o'clock.

5. Why does the man mean when he says: 'we will have to get up earlier and leave home earlier'?

A. It will take him longer to travel to school because of traffic police.
B. The roads will be more congested because of more exits.
C. He expects the next year's classes to begin earlier.
D. The man thinks construction will cause traffic delays.

ANSWER: D. The man thinks construction will cause traffic delays.

Answer A can be discarded because there is no indication of traffic police directing traffic. The text specifically states that there will be fewer exits, so Answer B is incorrect. The man does not discuss the schedule for next year. D is the correct answer because he believes that narrower exits and fewer exits will cause traffic delays. Thus, he must leave home earlier so he won't be late.

6. According to the text, what is flan?

A. A cooked banana.
B. An appetizer.
C. A dessert.
D. Heaven in your mouth

Answer: C. a dessert
The woman explains that flan is a baked custard or pudding made with eggs and a caramel syrup. Custards are served after the main meal as desserts.

7. What does the man's favorite sport?

   A. Soccer
   B. Football
   C. Cycling
   D. Basketball

Answer: C. Cycling.
Another word for bicycle riding as a sport is cycling.

8. Why does the woman find it difficult to do her job at the restaurant well?

   A. Because her boss is very demanding.
   B. Because she has a poor memory.
   C. Because the boss is always complaining.
   D. Because they get very busy at times.

Answer: D. Because they get very busy at times.
The woman finds it difficult because her boss is demanding and it is hard to remember everything when they are so busy.

LISTENING

Part 3

(Narrator) Listen to part of a lecture in a science class.

(Male professor) Today I'm going to talk about the small world of machines. In the past, machines were unable to work at a micro- (or tiny) scale. For example, doctors did not have tools that allowed them to repair the body from the inside. Plumbers did not have any way to locate broken pipes deep inside a building. Now, things are changing. Computers and biophysics are creating a new world where scientists can build microscopic machines. This is the exciting world of nanotechnology.

Just look at some of the uses of nanotechnology.

- A probe that provides images of a patient's arteries is being used in cardiology centers around the world.
- A product which uses nanoparticles to clean glass by breaking down dirt particles and wash them away when water comes in contact with the glass.
- Clothing that contains a thin layer of zinc oxide to protect against UV radiation.
- Scratch resistant polymer coatings that contain aluminum silicate nanoparticles making earlier polymer coatings more effective by increasing resistance to chipping and scratching.
- Bandages that incorporate nanoparticles of silver ions to block harmful bacteria's ability to breath.

Nanotechnology is producing new products every day. Many exciting medical applications have been invented, but nanotechnology isn't limited to the field of medicine. In the world of tennis, Wilson has created a tennis ball with a double core. The inner core has a coating of clay nanoparticles that makes it very difficult for air to escape from the ball. The tennis racket has been engineered with nanotube-infused graphite. This creates a very light racket many times stronger than steel.

Yet, all of these advances have challenges and risks, too. Scientists need to learn more about how atoms join together to create larger structures. On a smaller scale, a nanoscale, elements act differently than in larger groups. Some scientists believe that nanoparticles could be dangerous to humans even toxic. They fear that the nanoparticles could pass from the bloodstream into the brain.

Tomorrow's lecture will concern the ethics of nanotechnology. Is it ethical to create a race of humans that are enhanced by nanotechnology? Is it ethical to build stronger and more lethal weapons? What will happen to manufacturing jobs if nanotechnology eliminates the need for them? These are just some of the questions we will discuss in tomorrow's class.

[**SOURCE:** Bonsor, K & Strickland, J. How Nanotechnology Works. http://science.howstuffworks.com/nanotechnology.htm]

1. What is the lecture mainly about?

A. Innovations in nanotechnology
B. A comparison of nanotechnology and previous technology.
C. The ethics of nanotechnology
D. Problems with nanotechnology.

ANSWER: A. Innovations in nanotechnology
The lecture does not discuss previous technology so comparisons cannot be made. The ethics of nanotechnology is the subject of the following lecture. Problems with nanotechnology are mentioned briefly. The main emphasis of the lecture is how nanotechnology is affecting our lives in many different ways through innovative technology. Answer A is the correct choice.

2. In what way is nanotechnology different from previous technology?

A. It is smaller.
B. It is microscopic.
C. It is larger.
D. It is huge.

ANSWER B. It is microscopic.
The lecture describes nanotechnology as tiny or micro-. The correct choice is B.

3. According to the professor, which one of the following options is an actual nanotechnology product in use today?

A. Clothing that can wash itself.
B. Bandages that kill bacteria by eliminating their food source.
C. Scratch-proof paint for cars.
D. Glass that can clean itself.

ANSWER: D. Glass that can clean itself.

The lecture talks about clothing that can help block UV radiation not wash itself. Bandages that have silver ion nanoparticles kill bacteria by blocking their ability to breathe. Scratch-proof polymer that contains aluminum silicate to increase the resistance to chipping and scratching is mentioned, but its application is not discussed. The correct answer is D. Glass that can clean itself.

4. In his next class, the professor will lecture about all of the following EXCEPT

- A. Creating a new race of humans
- B. The economics of nanotechnology
- C. The ethics of more lethal weapons
- D. The need for smaller medical devices

Answer: D. The need for smaller medical devices

The professor said he would talk about ethics in his next class. Ethics is a part of options A, B, and C.

Listen to the following presentation by a school guidance counselor. Then, answer the questions.

Good morning. I wanted to talk to you about applying for the college or university of your choice. There are many factors to be considered.

First of all, your grades are very important. Many colleges won't even consider new students with poor grades. However, if your tests, such as the IELTS, are very good, then they will compare your grades and the tests to make a decision.

Secondly, your after school activities are important. These are important because they show what your interests are when you can choose what you want to do. The admissions officers want to know if you worked or gave your time to help others. Were you interested in sports?

Finally, there're scholarships. Sometimes, if you are very good in sports, any sport, you might be eligible for a sports scholarship. However, sports scholarships aren't the only ones available. There are scholarships for almost anything you want to study: chemistry, English, and even, home economics. There are scholarships for the children of certain ethnic groups and for the children of previous students of the institution.

To conclude, I want to invite you to set up an appointment with me to discuss your options. My office is open from 8 – 10 for short questions like setting up appointments. I try to keep the afternoon hours open for longer appointments, but come to see me. We will work something out; I try to accommodate everyone.

Thank you for your attention.

5. What is the main idea of the talk?

    A. The counselor wants everyone to go to college.
    B. The counselor is discussing the factors college admissions officer study use in the admissions process.
    C. Factors to be considered in applying to college.
    D. How to get a scholarship

Answer: C. Factors to be considered in applying to college.
At the beginning of her talk, the counselor states the topic of her presentation. C is the correct option.

6. What does the counselor say is the most import factor in the admissions process?

    A. Grades
    B. Scholarships
    C. Test scores
    D. Sports

Answer: A. Grades.
The counselor begins with grades and says some colleges won't even consider students with poor grades. A is the correct option.

7. Part of the conversation is repeated below. Read it and answer the question.

   We will work something out; I try to accommodate everyone.

What does the counselor mean by this statement?

   A. She is flexible and will try to adjust her schedule to the student's.
   B. She will help the student get into college.
   C. She tries to make appointments for all the school personnel.
   D. She wants to be helpful.

Answer: A. She is flexible and will try to adjust her schedule to the student's.
The counselor is talking about the students coming to see her for an appointment. The phrase 'we will work something out' means that she can make adjustments to her schedule if she can or it is necessary. A is the best option.

8. According to the presentation, what does the counselor say about scholarships? *Choose 2 answers.*
   A. Many different types of scholarships are available.
   B. There are many sports scholarship.
   C. It is hard to get a good scholarship.
   D. Academic scholarships are harder to get than sports scholarships.

Answers: A. Many different types of scholarships are available. AND B. There are many sports scholarship.
The counselor talked about both A and B, but she did not say that it was difficult to get a scholarship or that academic ones were harder to get than sports ones.

Listen the teacher talking about essays in a writing class.

(Professor) Today, I want to talk about essays. Many writers find essays difficult to write, but some of our greatest writers have been essayists. They take their ideas and write their opinion on a subject and explain why it should be important to us.

E. B. White is a good example. White wrote an essay called "The Hen: An Appreciation." It was written in 1944 during the Second World War and is pretty famous. In his essay, he talks about such things as showing the hens respect, and "her elegance and girlish ways". Who talks about chickens that way? No one I know!

Essays were a pretty dull and unappreciated form of writing at first, but later, according to the Oxford Companion to the English Language, became "reflective, elegant, and philosophical". We can see all three qualities in White's essay. He is elegant in describing the attributes of the hens. He is philosophical when he discusses the difficulties he faced over long periods of time with his hens. He claims their relationship was "not easy to maintain". And finally, he is reflective throughout the piece. He says, "Chickens do not always enjoy an honorable position among city-bred people, although the egg, I notice, goes on and on."

I urge you to read the complete essay. It is a fine example of all the qualities expected in a good essay. Questions about will be on our next quiz, and you should be thoroughly familiar with it. Moving on.

9. How does the professor feel about studying White?

    A. He thinks it would be rewarding.
    B. He believes that it is useless.
    C. He says that it will be on the test.
    D. He believes studying essay writing is uninteresting.

Answer: A. He thinks it would be rewarding.
He believes studying essay writing is rewarding. The professor says "It is a fine example of all the qualities expected in a good essay."

10. The professor has all of the following reactions to the essay on hens EXCEPT

   A. He thinks it is humorous.
   B. He thinks it is an unusual subject.
   C. He believes it follows the rules of a good essay
   D. He believes the subject of the essay is inappropriate.

Answer: D. He believes the subject of the essay is inappropriate.
The professor believes that the subject is unusual (Who talks about chickens that way? No one I know!), but humorous. He also believes essay completes all the requirements of a good essay (It is a fine example…).

11. What does the professor say about early essays? *Choose 2 answers.*

   A. They were not valued.
   B. They were philosophical.
   C. They were exciting.
   D. They were unimaginative.

Answer: A. They were not valued AND D. They were unimaginative.
The professor says that they were pretty dull (unimaginative) and unappreciated (not valued).

12. What is the lecture mainly about?

   A. The history of the essay
   B. E. B. White's contributions to the essay
   C. An analysis of White's essay on "The Hen"
   D. The essay

Answer: D. The essay
The lecture is not about the history of the essay. It only talks about the beginnings of the essay briefly and stops with White's work in the 1940s. While B, White's contributions to the essay are discussed, the professor is using the essay as an example, but not analyzing it completely. The best choice would be Option D The essay. The lecture gives a brief analysis of its form and one example of a good essay.

Reading Answers

Reading Comprehension
-50 questions about reading passages

Part 3

Reading Comprehension

Directions: Read the passage. Then answer the questions.

1	No one knows exactly how chocolate was discovered. Approximately, one thousand years ago, somewhere in Central America, the Mayan Indians began to roast the odd shaped fruit and use the seeds in a drink called *chocolatl* or *xocoatl*. This "bitter water" has evolved into what we know today as hot chocolate.
2	Historians believe that the way to use and enjoy the cocoa fruit was discovered over 2500 years ago. The fruit was probably used for the pulp which was slightly acidic. Later the beans or seeds were roasted and **pulverized** to make a thick, **coarse** paste. This paste was flavored with different seeds, vanilla, chilies and honey. After the paste was flavored, it was allowed to dry. The chocolate paste became hard and could easily be transported by the natives in rectangular shapes called tablets. The natives used the chocolate tablets to make a drink by dissolving the tablets in water and whipping it until frothy.
3	Columbus discovered chocolate on his fourth trip to the Americas. He did not like the drink as prepared by the natives. Yet, he realized the beans were valuable to the Mayans because they rushed to pick up some beans that fell when the Spaniards were loading their ship with **them**. He carried some beans back to King Ferdinand V of Spain who was not impressed with them at first.
4	Hernan Cortez discovered also the value of the cocoa beans when he found Moctezuma's treasury. He had expected to find gold, but instead he found more than one billion cocoa beans. The Spaniard realized they were valuable, but he wasn't sure exactly how.
5	Cortez learned how to prepare chocolate and carried his knowledge back to Spain where it remained unpopular. In 1530 and 1540, the nuns at the Guanaco convent in South America began adding sugar and vanilla to the drink. This made the drink more popular to the European palate.
6	For almost 100 years, Spain and her colonies maintained a **monopoly** on the cocoa beans. In 1606, the monopoly ended and other European nations began to obtain the cocoa beans and produce chocolate.
7	The cocoa beverage became very popular in Europe through the royal courts and the nobility. Chocolate houses were the rage, yet the drink would probably not appeal to us today. The drink was thick, acrid, and greasy.
8	Many attempts were made to eliminate the bitterness and oiliness by adding wheat, corn or oat flour. Nothing worked until Coenraad van Houten invented a hydraulic press that could extract two thirds of the fat. The press had two great advantages. It could eliminate most of the fat which could be used to make chocolate for eating, and it could use the remains of the paste for grinding into cocoa powder. The alkalizing process, called *dutching*, allowed the powder to remain suspended in liquids for longer periods of time.
9	The manufacture of modern chocolate candy began over 150 years ago in Sweden by the Swiss brothers Cloetta who built their Steam-Chocolate-Factory in the city of Malmo. When

	another Swiss discovered how to manufacture milk solids, the milk chocolate candy bar was created.
10	In modern times, chocolate **confections** became a billion dollar industry. The world's biggest consumer of chocolate is Switzerland with an average of 19.8 pounds per person followed by Germany at 17.4 pounds. The United States comes in ninth on this chart with only 9.5 pounds per person. According to Statista in 2016, worldwide chocolate confectionery consumption was a staggering 7.3 million tons in 2015-2016. Milk chocolate is the preferred flavor with over 50% of the market.
11	Even though cocoa beans were discovered in the Americas, more than two-thirds of the world's production comes from West Africa. The largest company in the world that manufactures and sells chocolate and cocoa products is Barry Callebaut. This wholesaler, a business-to-business (b2b) entity, produces chocolate that appears in one of five products around the world. About 42% and 26% of their chocolate products are sold to Europe and America respectively of an astonishing 1.8 million tonnes.
Sources	Young, A.M. The chocolate tree—a natural history of chocolate. Washington: Smithsonian Institute Press. Barry Callebaut website: https://www.barry-callebaut.com/at-a-glance

Directions: Answer the following questions.

1. The word "pulverized" in paragraph 2 is closest in meaning to

    A. carefully preserved
    B. decimated
    C. destroyed
    D. crushed

Answer: D. Crushed
The correct word choice is crushed (pressed or pounded) into a powder or dust.

2. The word "coarse" in paragraph 2 is closest in meaning to

    A. rough
    B. consisting of large particles
    C. fine or delicate
    D. uneven

Answer: B. consisting of large particles
The correct word choice is 'consisting of large particles' the opposite of fine or delicate.

3. Which of the following made the tablets easy to transport?

   A. The tablets were hard and dry.
   B. The tablets were stackable.
   C. The tablets were small.
   D. The tablets were easily broken.

Answer: A. The tablets were hard and dry.
According to the paragraph 2, the tablets were hard and dry. The other factors were not mentioned in the text.

4. What can be inferred from paragraph 1 and 2 as reasons King Ferdinand V did not like the chocolate drink?

   A. The drink was not well prepared
   B. His friends did not like the drink either.
   C. The drink was bitter.
   D. The flavors were unusual.

Answer: C. The drink was bitter.
In paragraph 1, the drink was referred to as 'bitter water'. Even though the paste was 'flavored' with honey, apparently it still wasn't a sweet drink because it would probably not turn hard and dry if it had a lot of honey in the mixture.

5. What does the word them in paragraph 3 refer to?

   A. Beans
   B. Natives
   C. Mayans
   D. Ship

Answer: A. beans
The word 'them' refers back to the word 'beans', its antecedent even though there are many other nouns between the words them and beans.

6. What can be inferred from paragraph 4 about Cortez's discovery of the cocoa beans?

   A. He was probably disappointed.
   B. He was excited.
   C. He was elated about the discovery.
   D. He was saddened.

Answer: A. He was probably disappointed.
Cortez was expecting to find gold when he discovered Moctezuma's treasury. Gold was a known valuable element, but the value of cocoa beans was unknown. Cortez didn't not know why the natives valued these beans so much.

7. Select the TWO answer choices that are mentioned in paragraph 5 as being reasons chocolate became popular in the 1500s. *To receive credit, you must select TWO answers.*

   A. The nuns flavor the chocolate drink with vanilla.
   B. The nuns made the drink more popular to Europeans.
   C. The European palate was more refined.
   D. The drink had added sugar.

Answers: A. The nuns flavored the chocolate drink with vanilla AND D. The drink had added sugar.
The answers B and C are true statements but are not reasons the drink became more popular. A and D are the correct answer choices.

8. The word 'monopoly' in paragraph 6 is closest in meaning to

   A. exclusive control
   B. right to sell in large quantities
   C. ability to exploit the market
   D. cartel

Answer: A. exclusive control
The word 'monopoly' is closets in meaning to A. exclusive control.

9. Select TWO answer choices mentioned in paragraph 8 as being reasons the hydraulic press improved the processing of chocolate. To receive credit, you must select TWO answers.

   A. It could eliminate most of the chocolate.
   B. It could eliminate most of the fat.
   C. It could use the remains of the paste.
   D. It could grind the beans into powder.

Answers: B. It could eliminate most of the fat AND C. It could use the remains of the paste. Paragraph 8 clearly states the reasons given in B and C. Answer A is the opposite of Answer B. Answer D mentions grinding whereas the hydraulic press means to apply steady force or weight.

10. **In paragraph 8, there is a missing sentence. The paragraph is repeated below and show four letters (A, B, C, and D) that indicate where the following sentence could be added.**

Van Houten also discovered how to neutralize the acidity of the product by using potash.

Many attempts were made to eliminate the bitterness and oiliness by adding wheat, corn or oat flour. **(A)** Nothing worked until Coenraad van Houten invented a hydraulic press that could extract two thirds of the fat. The press had two great advantages. **(B)** It could eliminate most of the fat which could be used to make chocolate for eating, and it could use the remains of the paste for grinding into cocoa powder. **(C)** The alkalizing process, called *dutching*, allowed the powder to remain suspended in liquids for longer periods of time. **(D)**

   A. Option A
   B. Option B
   C. Option C
   D. Option D

Answer: Option C.
The correct placement of the sentence places van Houten's discovery of neutralizing the acidity before an explanation of the process and its name.

11. The word 'confections' in paragraph 10 is closest in meaning to

   A. cakes
   B. candy
   C. desserts
   D. any type of sweet preparation

Answer: D. any type of sweet preparation
The term 'confections' is used to refer to all preparations that use chocolate in their preparation, not just candies.

12. In paragraph 10, which one of the following is **NOT** mentioned as a major statistic about chocolate?

   A. Worldwide chocolate consumption was 7.3 million tons in 2015-2016.
   B. Milk chocolate accounted for over 50% of the total consumption.
   C. The Swiss eat the most chocolate.
   D. The United States prefers milk chocolate to other types of chocolate.

Answer: D. The United States prefers milk chocolate to other types of chocolate.
This statement may be true, but it is not substantiated by the text. All other facts are mentioned in the text.

13. In paragraph 11, all of the following statements are mentioned EXCEPT

   A. 2/3 of the cocoa production comes from Central America.
   B. Barry Callehaut is the largest b2b chocolate company in the world.
   C. Callehaut sells about 42% of their products to Europe.
   D. Callehaut sells about 1.8 million tonnes to Europe and America annually.

Answer: A. 2/3 of the cocoa production comes from Central America
According to the text, approximately 2/3 of the cocoa production comes from West Africa. Statement A is false.

14. Directions: An introductory sentence for a brief summary of the passage is provided below. Complete the summary by selecting the THREE answer choices that express the most important ideas in the passage. Some sentences do not belong in the summary because they express ideas that are not presented in the passage or are minor ideas in the passage. *This question is worth 2 points.*

Write your answer choices in the spaces where they belong. You can either write the letter of your answer choice or you can copy the sentence.

Chocolate has grown in popularity over the years, but at first, it was not popular in Europe.
•
•
•

A. Chocolate was first discovered in the Americas about 2500 years ago.
B. Columbus and King Ferdinand V did not like chocolate at first.
C. Because of nun in the Guanaco convent, chocolate became more popular.
D. Today, chocolate is a billion dollar industry.
E. The hydraulic press extracted 2/3 of the fat making modern chocolate possible.
F. Cortez had a more important role in the popularization of chocolate than Columbus.

Answer:

Chocolate has grown in popularity over the years, but at first, it was not popular in Europe.	
•	A. Chocolate was first discovered in the Americas about 2500 years ago.
•	E. The hydraulic press extracted 2/3 of the fat making modern chocolate possible.
•	D. Today, chocolate is a billion dollar industry.

These three answers illustrate the different phases in the popularization of chocolate.

Directions: Read the passage. Then answer the questions.

	The African Violet
1	The history of the African violet is one where a species from Africa took the world by storm for many reasons. The violet was discovered in 1892 in the Usambara Mountains in Tanganyika (now Tanzania) by Baron Walter von Saint Paul. He sent seeds and maybe some plants to his father in Germany. The Director of the Royal Botanic Garden declared them a new **species**.
2	The plant was named *Saintpaulia ionantlia*. The *Saintpaulia* was to honor the discoverer of the plants. The Greek word ***ionantha*** means with violet like flowers. Many years later, another botanist discovered that there were actually two species in the plants sent to Germany by Baron von Saint Paul. This second species was named *Saintpaulia confusa*.
3	In 1893, the first African violets were shipped to a New York from Europe. Years later, the Armacost and Royston Nursery in Los Angeles obtained seeds from Germany and England. From their seedlings, the nursery selected ten plants became known as the original ten. These ten seedlings and two species plants have produced most of the over 18,000 registered plants in existence today through **hybridizing**.
4	Over the years, several more species plants were added to the original classification of the *Saintpaulia* and increased the known varieties to more than twenty. They were later reduced to six. However, modern DNA testing has entered the **fray** and in 2015, the species were listed as ten. Scientists studied their leaf structure, geographical location in the wild and their evolutionary development.
5	The work of scientists in classifying African violets might seem **frivolous** at first, but the plants are extremely valuable commercially. The information the scientific community gives commercial growers, who are constantly creating new hybrids, contributes to the violet's commercial success. In 2015, the potted flowering plants were valued at $714 million with California and Florida being the two biggest growers. While this figure is reflective of all flowering indoor plants, African violets were

a major player in this market. Commercial growers like African violets because they can produce a flowering plant in five to six weeks and because of the huge variety of plants. The African violet is called "America's favorite houseplant" for a reason!
Sources: Bartholomew, P. and AVSA. Growing to Show. Rev. 2008. Waterloo, Iowa. Pioneer graphics, 119 p.. Nishii, K. et al Streptocarpus redefined to include all Afro-Malagasy Gesneriaceae:... Taxon 64 (6) December 2015: 1243-1274. USAD. Floriculture Crops. 2015 Summary.

15. The word 'species' in paragraph 1 is closest in meaning to
    A. Plant
    B. A distinct kind
    C. Different color
    D. Flowering plant

Answer: B. a distinct kind
Species means a distinct kind, class, sort or variety.

16. Where does the word *Ionantha* in paragraph 2 come from

    A. Greek
    B. Germany
    C. Africa
    D. Europe

Answer: A. Greek
The word comes from the Greek and means with violet like flowers.

17. How did the African violet get the name *Saintpaulia*?

    A. From the native African culture.
    B. From the Greek
    C. From the last name of the discoverer
    D. From the Tanganyika language

Answer: C. From the last name of the discoverer

The name of the discoverer is often used to honor the person who discovered a new animal or plant species, as in this case.

18. The word 'hybridizing' in paragraph 3 is closest in meaning to

    A. Crossbreeding
    B. Mixing
    C. Purifying
    D. Detoxifying

Answer: A. Crossbreeding
To hybridize means to cross two different species or crossbreed. The process is usually used to produce newer and better plants or animals.

19. The word 'fray' in paragraph 4 is closest in meaning to

    A. Discussion
    B. Talks
    C. Conversation
    D. Brawl

Answer: D. Brawl
The word 'fray' indicates a brawl, that is, a noisy quarrel or fight.

20. According to paragraph 4, how did scientists determine the current number of species? *Choose 2 answers.*

    A. By studying taxonomy charts
    B. By studying the DNA of the plants
    C. By studying their geographical location in the wild
    D. By looking at plants and their characteristics

Answer: B. By studying the DNA of the plants AND C. By studying their geographical location in the wild.
According to paragraph 4, there has been many different classifications that have listed from 6 to 20 different species. The newest classification lists 10 species which scientists arrived at by testing the DNA and studying their geographical location in the wild.

21. Why is the scientific classification of the *Saintpaulia* important?

   A. It is an important commercial product.
   B. There is a huge number of varieties.
   C. Scientific knowledge satisfies our curiosity.
   D. The plants are easy to grow.

Answer: A. It is an important commercial product.
According to the text, the Saintpaulia is an important commercial product.

22. Write the letter or the sentence of the THREE (3) best answer choices that express the most important ideas of the passage. **This question is worth 2 points.**

The African violet is America's favorite houseplant for many reasons.
•
•
•

Choose 3 answers from the following choices.
1. African violets have many different hybrids.
2. African violets are a huge commercial success.
3. African violets are easy to grow.
4. Commercial growers can produce a crop in 5-6 weeks.
5. There are many more species that originally thought.
6. Flowering indoor plants, including African violets, are a huge economic market.

Answers: 1, 2, 3
Answers 1, 2, and 3 explain why African violets popular plants.

Reading Comprehension
Questions about reading passages
Nos. 23-50

Part 3_b

Reading Comprehension

Directions: Read the passage. Then answer the questions that follow the passage.

	MOUNTAINS
1	Mountains are all around us on the surface of the Earth and in the ocean's depths. They are caused by different types of movement of the Earth. Many mountains exist on each of the continents, but what are mountains? Geologists classify land masses of higher than 1,000 feet as mountains, and mountain close together as chains or mountain ranges.
2	Mountains often **function** as the boundaries between different countries (like the Pyrenees that separate Spain and Portugal) or mountains can act as a protective barrier that protect countries from invading armies. Switzerland has used their natural landscape to prevent invasions and to provide refuge for centuries. Because of the high Alps, Switzerland has remained neutral for most of its existence.
3	There are four main types of mountains: fault-block mountains (such as the Sierra Nevada in California), volcanic mountains (such as Mount St. Helens in Washington State), dome mountains (such as the Black Hills of South Dakota), and plateau mountains (such as mountains in New Zealand).
4	Simply explained, plate tectonics cause gigantic pieces of the Earth's crust to fold and **buckle** or break into blocks. Volcanic and fault-block mountains form when the plates collide with each other. The crust (also called lithosphere) 'floats' on the surface of the Earth. Beneath the lithosphere lies the asthenosphere, a layer of solid rock that **is subjected to** so much heat and pressure that is becomes liquid. If the asthenosphere pushes through the cracks and rises, it causes fault-block mountains. If the crust breaks into gigantic blocks; the blocks can move up and down and may stack on top of each other.
5	**Dome** mountains are formed when the magma rises up but doesn't break through the surface of the Earth's crust. As the dome hardens, it remains higher than the surrounding area and is worn away by wind and rain erosion. The mountains become more circular and have rounded tops.
6	Plateau mountains are formed in a way similar to dome mountains. The tectonic plates push up huge chunks of land, but without folding or faulting. These mountains are then formed by other elements such as erosion or **weathering**.
7	Mountains impact our lives and play. They affect our weather, the flow of water, and animal and plant life. When mountains are formed by volcanic eruptions, minerals are brought to the surface. Because many rivers begin in the high mountain peaks, mountains are good place to build electric power stations. Mountains provide the **site** for many winter sports, such as skiing and snowboarding. Since man cannot move mountains, he has learned to live with nature's landscape.
SOURCES	Barrow, M. The Mountain Environment. http://www.primaryhomeworkhelp.co.uk/mountains/types.htm

| | Mountains: highest points on Earth. http://science.nationalgeographic.com/science/earth/surface-of-the-earth/mountains-article |

23. This passage is mainly about

    A. How mountains are made
    B. Description of the different types of mountains
    C. How mountains function
    D. Description of mountains and their functions

Answer: D. Description of mountains and their functions

The passage describes mountains and their functions. Part of the description of mountains is how they are formed.

24. The word 'function' in paragraph 2 is closest in meaning to

    A. Act
    B. Goal
    C. Work
    D. Power

Answer: A. Act

The word function is closest in meaning to act.

25. In paragraph 2, all of the following are given as reasons mountains protect humans EXCEPT

    A. To establish borders between countries
    B. To deter enemies
    C. To provide recreation
    D. To prevent invading armies

Answer: C. To provide recreation

According to the text, mountains protect humans by providing security and borders between countries. Mountains are useful in providing recreation, but this does not protect us.

26. What can be inferred from the information in paragraphs 2 and 3 about mountains?

   A. Mountains are prevalent on Earth.
   B. Mountains are rare on the Earth's surface.
   C. Different types of mountains are formed in different locations on Earth.
   D. The Alps are domed mountains.

Answer: C. Different types of mountains are formed in different locations on Earth.
We can infer that different types of mountains are formed in different locations on Earth, because the examples used to illustrate different mountains are from different regions. The author doesn't illustrate two types of mountains with the same mountain or mountain ranges.

27. The word 'buckle' in paragraph 4 is closest in meaning to

   A. Yield
   B. Knuckle
   C. Bend
   D. Clasp

Answer: C. Bend
The word buckle, when used as a verb, means to bend.

28. The words 'is subjected to' in paragraph 4 are closest in meaning to

   A. Is removed from
   B. Undergoes
   C. Is vulnerable to
   D. Experiences

Answer: C. is vulnerable to
To subject an object or person to something suggests that they or it is vulnerable to something.

29. What is plate tectonics?

   A. Blocks of Earth that move
   B. Movement of pieces of the Earth's crust
   C. Explanation of how mountains are formed
   D. Volcanoes that form mountains

Answer: B. Movement of pieces of the Earth's crust
In its most simple form, plate tectonics is the movement of pieces of the Earth's crust.

30. Which of the following can be inferred from the description of plate tectonics in paragraph 4?

   A. Volcanic and fault-block mountains are formed in the same way.
   B. Any amount of force can cause a plate to collide with another plate
   C. Plates exist in only a few countries.
   D. The surface of the Earth is in constant motion.

Answer: D. The surface of the Earth is in constant motion.
Since the crust or lithosphere 'floats' on the surface of the Earth, we can infer that it is in constant motion because of the forces at work on the asthenosphere.

31. The word 'dome' in paragraph 5 is closest in meaning to

   A. Cupola
   B. Oval
   C. Ragged
   D. peaked

Answer: A. cupola
The word dome is closest in meaning to the architectural structure, cupola.

32. The word 'weathering' in paragraph 6 is closest in meaning to

    A. effects of natural elements on a mountain
    B. physical effects on land surfaces
    C. chemical effects on mountains
    D. changed by rain

Answer: A. effects of natural elements on a mountain
Since the passage is discussing mountains, the correct answer is a. the effects of natural elements on a mountain. This would include both the physical and chemical effects of nature.

33. The word 'site' in paragraph 7 is closest in meaning to

    A. sitting room
    B. place
    C. resort
    D. land

Answer: B. place
The word 'site' means place, location or venue.

34. In paragraph 7 of the passage, a sentence is missing. Look at the paragraph, which is repeated below, and choose one of the four letters (A, B, C, and D) to indicate where the following sentence could be added.

Because many rivers begin in the high mountain peaks, mountains are good place to build electric power stations.

Mountains impact our lives and play. They affect our weather, the flow of water, and animal and plant life. (A) When mountains are formed by volcanic eruptions, minerals are brought to the surface. (B) Mountains provide the <u>site</u> for many winter sports, such as skiing and snowboarding. (C) Since man cannot move mountains, he has learned to live with nature's landscape. (D)

    A. Option A
    B. Option B
    C. Option C
    D. Option D

Answer: Option B.

35. **Directions: In the following table, a sentence is provided to introduce a summary of the passage. Choose THREE more sentences from the sentences below to complete your summary. Some of the sentences given are not included in the passage or are minor ideas from the passage.** *The question is worth 2 points.*

Write your answers in the space below. You can just write the letter of the sentence or copy the whole sentence.

Mountains are formed by powerful geological forces and mankind has learned how to use them to his advantage.
•
•
•

Answer Choices

A. Mountains have many functions in the development of different countries.

B. Plate tectonics can be used to explain how mountains are formed.

C. Dome mountains are formed by magma.

D. Weathering shapes plateau mountains.

E. Mountains determine how we work and many of our sports.

F. Natural forces shape the Earth.

Answers: A, B, and E.
Sentences C and D talk about only two kinds of mountains. Sentence F talks about natural forces, but there are many natural forces not mentioned in the passage, such as gravity and magnetism of the poles.

Directions: Read the passage below. Then answer the questions that follow the passage.

1	Positive psychology is a relatively new branch of psychology. It can be defined as the scientific study of happiness or as the study of the strengths that enable people and communities to succeed. Positive psychology tries to explain and understand happiness and well-being. Throughout history, mankind has looked for explanations for these human **traits**. Socrates said, "The secret of change is to focus all of your energy, not on fighting the old, but on building the new." He believed in knowing oneself.
2	Despite the long history of happiness, psychologists dwelt on digging into people's pasts, **ferreting out** their secrets, and analyzing minute details of their pasts. Positive psychology is just the opposite. It emphasizes the importance building on the positive aspects of people's lives and helping them enjoy their present and having hope for a happy future.
3	Positive psychology was first proposed in 1998 by Martin Seligman, a University of Pennsylvania psychologist. In his address to the American Psychological Association, he started a new movement in psychology by **exhorting** his fellow psychologists to "turn toward understanding and building the human strengths to complement our emphasis on healing damage." In his book *Flourish: A Visionary New Understanding of Happiness and Well-being (2011)*, Seligman expanded his theory to include positive relationships and accomplishments.
4	Positive psychology has since focused on three areas of human **endeavor**: positive emotions, positive individual traits and positive institutions. To develop positive emotions, people must be content with their past, happy in the present and hopeful for the future. The individual's positive traits come from his or her individual strengths and virtues. Positive institutions focus on how to improve a community by utilizing its strengths.
5	We don't need to be happy or joyful all the time. Happiness is not a response to dangerous situations. We need a range of emotions to help protect us from dangerous—fight or flight—situations. We need happiness and joy to compensate for the negative emotions in order to live a positive life as we **seek** happiness. Joy is the ultimate response that we can experience, but we can't sustain it for long. Joy is **fleeting**.
6	Another key to positive change is positive relationships. Married couples are happier than single people. Researchers debate the reasons why, but the fact remains that happily married couples live longer, have better social skills, and are healthier.
7	Strong and healthy social ties are another key to positive living. The Framingham Heart Study found that happiness and unhappiness tended to spread through close relationships. Researchers found that happiness spread more consistently than unhappiness through the network. Having a good friend helps people **cushion** the impact of negative life experiences, and thus, increases one's self-esteem. Social interactions, such as a gift of flowers, may affect a wide variety of emotions.
8	Age does matter. Researchers have shown that during their 20s and 70s, individuals are happier than during the decades of the 40s and 50s. The reasons are not entirely clear, but some facts stand out. After the 20s, feelings of stress and anger decline. Perhaps it is because certain social skills take time to develop or perhaps it is because hormones become more stabilized. Older people have more health problems, but fewer problems in general.
9	Money cannot buy happiness according to the old **saying**. Research seems to support this

10	adage. Money is important to the poor who have not met their basic needs, but less so to the middle class and the wealthy. Lottery winners have higher levels of happiness immediately after winning, but the happiness level soon drops and returns to previous levels within a short period of time.
10	Personality plays an important part in our happiness. **Genetics** play a role in our personality and the emotions associated with personality. Neuroscientists believe that genetics control approximately 80% of our long-term sense of well-being leaving 20% that can be influenced by the environment and learning from sources such as positive change.
11	Many researchers believe that individual differences are important, but research to date suggests that most people will benefit from the **doctrines** of Positive Psychology. Psychologists will continue to develop new techniques and exercises to improve our daily lives, and this is good. All human experience moves forward by experimenting, discarding the things that don't work well and accepting new challenges.

36. What is the main idea of the passage?

    A. Positive Psychology is good for us.
    B. Positive Psychology is a new field.
    C. What is Positive Psychology?
    D. An explanation of Seligman's theory.

Answer: B. Positive Psychology is a new field.
The passage discusses the new field of Positive Psychology and explains some elements of the theory. It does not offer an explanation of Seligman's theory, i.e. what he said in his speech to the American Psychological Association not does it summarize what he wrote about in his book, *Flourish*.

37. The word 'traits' in paragraph 1 is closest in meaning to

    A. Quantity
    B. Individual
    C. Quality
    D. Ideology

Answer: C. quality
The word traits mean characteristic or quality.

38. The words 'ferreting out' in paragraph 2 is closest in meaning to

   A. secreting
   B. searching for
   C. disguising
   D. suppressing

Answer: B. searching for
The expression ferreting out means hunting, looking for, or searching for.

39. The word 'exhorted' in paragraph 3 is closest in meaning to

   A. Impeded
   B. Absolved
   C. Deterred
   D. Urged

Answer: D. urged
The word exhorted means to admonish strongly or to urge someone to do something.

40. All of the following are mentioned in paragraph 4 as elements of Positive Psychology EXCEPT

   A. Positive emotions
   B. Positive institutions
   C. Positive communities
   D. Positive individual traits

Answer: C. positive communities
Positive communities come from strengthening positive institutions. The words are not used as synonyms, but rather as institutions which improve communities such as a nursing home community, a school community, or a community of elder citizens.

41. The word 'fleeting' in paragraph 5 is closest in meaning to

   A. Short-lived
   B. Persistent
   C. Lasting
   D. Enduring

Answer: A. short-lived
The word fleeting means swift, rapid, or short-lived.

42. The word 'cushion' in paragraph 7 is closest in meaning to

   A. Harden
   B. An object to sit on
   C. Absorb
   D. Encircle

Answer: C. absorb
In this sentence, cushion means anything used to absorb shock, lessen the impact of something negative or that provides comfort. An examples would be steam in certain machines..

43. Which of the following is NOT mentioned in paragraph 7 as a reason that social ties are important?

   A. Good friends lessen the impact of negative life experiences.
   B. Good friends increase a person's self-esteem.
   C. Social interactions may affect a wide variety of emotions.
   D. Happiness is easier to spread than unhappiness in social networks.

Answer: B. Good friends increase a person's self-esteem.
According to paragraph 7, having good friends help people deal with negative life experiences (i.e. death, divorce, loss of a job, etc.), and therefore, dealing with these problems in a positive way increases one's self-esteem.

44. All of the following are mentioned in paragraph 8 as reasons why age matters in happiness EXCEPT

   A. Hormones settle down after the 20s.
   B. Older people have fewer problems in general.
   C. Older people don't have problems getting around.
   D. Stress and anger decline in the 20s.

Answer: C. Older people don't have problems getting around.
The paragraph discusses the reasons for different age groups becoming happier as they age. The ability of older people is lessened because some have problems moving around as they age. C is the best choice.

45. The word 'saying' in paragraph 9 is closest in meaning to

   A. Talking
   B. Sawyer
   C. Spreading
   D. Proverb

Answer: D. Proverb
A saying is a proverb or adage.

46. What can be inferred from paragraph 9 about money and happiness?

   A. Money can't buy happiness.
   B. The poor are happier.
   C. The middle class have their basic needs met.
   D. The wealthy are very happy.

Answer: C. The middle class have their basic needs met.
According to the paragraph, the middle class and the wealthy find money important, but not as much as the poor who do not have their basic needs met. Once the basic needs are met, money becomes less important to happiness.

47. The word 'genetics' in paragraph 10 is closest in meaning to

   A. Branch of biology
   B. Study of history
   C. Family
   D. Relatives

Answer: A. branch of biology
Genetics is a branch of biology that studies the origin of something.

48. The word 'doctrines' in paragraph 11 is closest in meaning to

   A. Evidence
   B. Documentation
   C. Stubborn
   D. Dogmas

Answer: D. dogmas
Doctrines mean the teachings, the beliefs, or the dogmas.

49. In paragraph 10, a sentence has been left out. The paragraph is repeated below and shows four letters (A, B, C, D) that indicate where the sentence below could be added.

Extroverts seem to be happier and perhaps this is because they develop stronger relationships and have more support groups than introverts.

(A) Personality plays an important part in our happiness. **(B) Genetics** play a role in our personality and the emotions associated with personality. **(C)** Neuroscientists believe that genetics control approximately 80% of our long-term sense of well-being leaving 20% that can be influenced by the environment and learning from sources such as positive change. **(D)**

   A. Option A
   B. Option B
   C. Option C
   D. Option D

Answer: B. Option B

Option B is the correct choice because the sentence is discussing a personality type—extroverts.

50. Directions: An beginning sentence for a short summary of the passage is given below. Complete the summary by choosing THREE answer choices that express the most important ideas in the passage. Some of the sentences may present ideas not presented in the passage or are minor details. *This question is worth 2 points.*

You may write the letter of your choice or you can copy your sentence in the spaces below.

Positive Psychology is a new branch of psychology.
•
•
•

Answer Choices

A. According to Positive Psychology, we can determine our own happiness.

B. Positive Psychology has focused on three areas of human endeavor.

C. Positive Psychology was the brain-child of an unknown psychologist.

D. We don't have to be happy all the time.

E. Factors, such as health, wealth, and social status, are important in our happiness level.

F. Money, age, and personality are factors that are an important part of our happiness.

Answers: A, B, E.
The best choices are A, B, E.

Structure & Expression Answers

Structure and Written Expression
-15 exercises of completing sentences correctly
-25 exercises of identifying errors

Structure and Written Expression

Part 1

Complete the following sentences.

1. None of the food _____ fresh.

A. tastes
B. were
C. tasting
D. taste

Answer: A. tastes
After the word 'none', the verb is always singular (tastes).

2. I have seen _____ interesting movies recently.

A. some
B. the
C. any
D. an

Answer: A. some
Some is used with plural countable nouns.

3. I congratulated the manager _____ his new promotion.

A. for
B. by
C. at
D. on

Answer: D. on
The preposition 'on' can be used to express 'with regard to'.

4. You're studying chemistry, _____ you?

A. are
B. was
C. aren't
D. do

Answer: C. aren't

When forming tag questions, a positive statement requires a negative tag for confirmation or when making conversation. The correct tag would be 'aren't you.'

5. Jane has a bad cold. She _____ better see a doctor.
A. should
B. had
C. ought
D. ought to

Answer: B. had

The expression 'had better' is informal and used to give advice to others. It is rarely used in formal writing.

6. The Mississippi river is a waterway _____ is used to carry boats with goods and passengers.

A. who
B. whom
C. which
D. that

Answer: D. that

'That' introduces essential adjective clauses and is the correct choice.

7. Yesterday, I went to the movies. I had a soda and a hot dog. I still wanted _____ ice cream when we got out.

A. some
B. no
C. any
D. few

Answer: A. some

In sentences with noncount nouns, you use the adjective some to modify the nouns in affirmative sentences. Any is used in negative sentences.

8. I get my exercise by running, cycling, and _____.

A. swimming
B. to play soccer
C. I have taken classes of tennis
D. being a boxer

Answer: A. swimming

The sentence needs another gerund, swimming, to complete the parallel structure of ways in which the speaker gets exercise.

9. Our coach gave us _____ because we couldn't settle down after we lost the football game.

A. some criticism
B. a hard time
C. a shout
D. a thing or two

Answer: B. a hard time

To complete the idiom, use the words 'a hard time' which mean 'scold' or 'complained'.

10. The study on cancer is showing how new technologies are improving cancer treatments. _____a major study conducted by the Mayo Clinic.

A. Its
B. Its'
C. Its is
D. It's

Answer: D. It's

The correct answer is D. It's. The sentence requires a subject and a verb as represented by the contraction of It is or It's.

11. If you meet me by four, we _____ to the movies at five.

A. go
B. will go
C. went
D. have gone

Answer: B. will go

If the present tense is used in the "if-clause", the future tense is used in the result clause. Therefore, option B is correct.

12. I _____ the football stadium from my balcony.

A. will see
B. can see
C. might see
D. had seen

Answer: B. can see
The verb can is often used with verbs of the five senses: see, hear, feel, smell, and taste or to express physical ability. B is the correct option.

13. Hamlet _____ by Shakespeare.

A. had been written
B. has been written
C. was written
D. is written

Answer: C. was written
The simple past of the verb write in the passive voice is 'was written' and the correct choice.

14. _____ you paid for the tickets to the movie, I will pay for the sodas and popcorn.

A. Now that
B. Because of
C. But
D. Since

Answer: D. Since
The adverb 'since' means 'because' and is the correct choice for the introductory clause.

15. I had promised my mom _____ my room after I took my shower.

A. cleaning
B. to look at
C. to clean up
D. washing

Answer: C. to clean up

The speaker would promise his or her mom 'to clean up' the room, not to look at it. The verb promise requires an infinitive after it so Options A and D can be discarded.

Part 2

Directions: In this section of the test, you will read a series of short texts created by nonnative English speakers. You will be asked to identify the errors in the students' writing.

Questions 1 – 3 are based on the following text about a popular sport in the student's native country.

Cycling of the world is a very popular sport in every country. Cyclists must has the skill to ride a bicycle without stopping for many miles. They train every day so that he can become world class racers.

1. In the first sentence, the error is in the relative order of:

A. A noun and an adjective
B. The direct and indirect object
C. The subject and object
D. The prepositional phrases

Answer: D. The prepositional phrases
The error lies in the order of the first two prepositional phrases. The sentence should read: Cycling is a very popular sport in every country of the world. Prepositional phrases normally are placed close to the words they modify. In this example, 'of the world' modifies country not cycling.

2. In sentence two, there is an error in:

A. Agreement between noun and verb
B. Pronoun and antecedent
C. Structure of the subordinate clause
D. Order of the sentence elements

Answer: A. Agreement between noun and verb
The noun 'Cyclists' does not agree in number with the verb 'has'. The correct form would be 'Cyclists must have...'

3. In the last sentence, there is an error in the:

A. Noun and an adjective
B. Direct and indirect objects
C. Subject and the object
D. Pronoun form

Answer: D. Pronoun form

In the last sentence, the antecedent of they is cyclists. Therefore, the plural form of the subject (nominative) pronoun should be used in the phrase so that they can become world class racers.

Questions 4-6 are based on an excerpt from an essay describing the student's favorite foods.

My favorite food for breakfast is a bread and a cheese with a cup of coffee and milk. In my country we eat a lot of beef. There is always any kind of rice at every meal, too. For snacks, we eat meat pastries called empanadas. Tourists in my country likes to eat fruit or a small square of guava paste for dessert.

4. In the first sentence, there is an error in the:

A. Verb tense
B. Parallel structure
C. Punctuation
D. Subject and object

Answer B: Parallel structure
The items in this series, (...a bread and a cheese with a cup of coffee and milk), should all have the same structure. The sentence should read: is a piece of bread, a piece or slice of cheese, and a cup of coffee and milk. In this case, the parallel structure is a noun with a prepositional phrase modifying it. The correct option is B.

5. In sentence number three, the word any is incorrect because:

A. Some is used with count nouns
B. Any is used with noncount nouns
C. Any is used in questions
D. Any is used in negative statements

Answer: A. Some is used with count nouns
Answers B, C, and D are correct about the use of any. Both some and any can be used with count nouns, but the meaning is different. Any in this sentence suggests that there is some kind of rice, but it doesn't specify what kind. In this sentence, some is used to express the idea of an unspecified kind of rice such as brown rice, white rice, rice with vegetables, etc. The correct answer is A.

6. In the last sentence, the correct form of the verb likes should be:

A. like
B. liked
C. will like
D. have liked

Answer: A. like

The writer is discussing what visitors enjoy eating always. Therefore, the simple present of the very is used. It should agree with the subject tourists, and thus must be the plural form of the verb. Answer A is the correct choice.

Answer the questions following each text.

7. I am studying Computer Science. I have the second semester.
The verb was in the second sentence is incorrect with respect to:

A. Tense
B. Gender
C. Person
D. Number

Answer: A. Tense

The pronoun I is not gender specific, so it may be used for both male and female people. The use of was for first person singular is correct in both person and number. However, when discussing current situations, the present tense am (in) is the correct tense. Thus, A is the correct answer.

8. I love my boyfriend too much.
The adverb too is incorrect with regards to:

A. Word order
B. Form
C. Spelling
D. Usage

Answer: D. Usage

The word order, form and spelling are all correct. Option D must be the incorrect form. The correct word in this case would be the adverb very. Choice D Usage is the correct answer.

9. My baby sister causes <u>much</u> problems every day.
The word <u>much</u> is incorrect because:

A. It is used with countable nouns.
B. It is used with no count nouns.
C. It is used with collective nouns.
D. It is used with compound nouns.

Answer: A. It is used with no count nouns.
The problem is using the adjective much with a countable when it is only used with no count (uncountable) nouns.

10. The football game started on time, but we were late getting <u>their</u>.
The word <u>their</u> is incorrect because:

A. <u>Their</u> is a possessive adjective used to indicate place.
B. <u>Their</u> is singular and should be plural.
C. <u>Their</u> is a preposition.
D. <u>Their</u> is a personal pronoun.

Answer: A. Their is a possessive adjective used to indicate place
The sentence states that the people were arriving at a place, so a noun or noun substitute, not an adjective, should be used in the sentence.

11. The beer in these glasses are bitter.
The word are is incorrect because:

A. The verb <u>are</u> is correct
B. The verb <u>are</u> should come after the subject beer.
C. The verb <u>are</u> is incorrect because the subject is beer.
D. The verb <u>are</u> is in the present tense and should be in the past.

Answer: C. The verb <u>are</u> is incorrect because the subject is beer.
The subject of the sentence is beer and the verb should agree with the subject in person and number. The subject is not glasses. Therefore, the verb should agree in number with the subject beer and should be the verb <u>is</u>.

In the following section, there may be an error in grammar, usage, word choice, or idioms. Parts of the sentence may be underlined. All other parts of the sentence are correct. Select the underlined word or words that are incorrect. Mark the incorrect answer on your answer sheet.

12. My favorite teacher is the <u>only</u> person <u>who</u> is completely qualified to teach <u>English</u> literature <u>to</u> high
          A   B   C   D

school.

Answer: D. to
The preposition <u>at</u> is used to indicate an area or place. The preposition <u>to</u>, in this case, should be used to indicate that the teacher will be teaching to someone (high school <u>students</u>), not a place (high school).

13. <u>When</u> the new Congress <u>took</u> office, legislation that <u>had been</u> ignored for years <u>is</u> urgent.
  A   B   C   D

Answer: D. is.
The verb tenses should all be in the past. <u>Became</u> would be the correct verb tense.

14. The <u>coup</u> in Turkey <u>failed</u> when the government <u>overcome</u> the <u>rebellious</u> military.
   A   B   C   D

Answer: C. overcome
The verbs should agree in tense. Overcome should be the past tense <u>overcame</u>.

15. Neither snow <u>or</u> hail <u>will keep</u> postmen from their <u>appointed</u> <u>rounds</u>.
       A   B   C   D

Answer: A. or
The preposition neither should be followed by the negative <u>nor</u> not or.

16. Some people <u>prefer</u> vanilla, <u>others</u> <u>prefer</u> chocolate. I prefer the <u>later</u>.
        A   B C   D

Answer: D
The word is spelled incorrectly. The word <u>later</u> means after some period of time. The word <u>latter</u> refers to the second word in a selection or chocolate.

17. She worked <u>during</u> the summer <u>not</u> because she <u>was needing</u> the money, <u>but</u> because she wanted
                           A   B   C   D
the experience.

Answer: C. was needing
The error is in parallelism. The sentence should read 'not because she needed the money' so that it agrees with 'because she wanted'.

18. The accident occurred <u>when</u> the school <u>bus,</u> carrying <u>students</u> overturned <u>on</u> the highway.
                                   A   B   C   D

Answer: B. bus,
In this sentence, the writer is emphasizing that only the bus carrying students overturned. Therefore, the phrase ",carrying students," should not be set off by a comma at the beginning (or at the end) of the phrase because it is essential information.

19. The crowds <u>wandered</u> along the streets slowly <u>taking in</u> the sight of vendors selling <u>they're</u> <u>wares</u>.
                   A   B   C   D

Answer: C. they're
The phrase <u>they're</u> wares is incorrect because it uses a subject and very contraction instead of the possessive adjective <u>their</u>.

20. The weather has been <u>very</u> hot. <u>However,</u> we have had three <u>weeks</u> of temperatures over 90
                              A   B   C
<u>degrees</u> Fahrenheit.
  D

Answer: B. However,
The adverbial conjunction "However," implies that " three weeks of temperatures over 90…" is in contrast to the preceding sentence. It isn't. It continues the idea of very hot weather. Therefore, "for example" would be a better choice of a transition word.

21. I enjoy visiting my grandmother on her birthday. <u>Some</u> of my <u>relatives</u> have returned <u>back</u> every year
                                                       A   B   C

for the <u>last</u> twenty-five years.
        D

Answer: C. back
All elements of these sentences are correct except 'back' which is redundant.

22. Exercise is a way to <u>improving</u> <u>your</u> <u>health,</u> especially if you do <u>it</u> often.
                              A   B   C   D

Answer: A. improving
The correct verb form after 'to' is the base form to create the infinitive. In this case, the correct word would be 'improve'.

23. John and I went <u>walking</u> on Saturday. <u>After</u> a few <u>blocks</u>, I ask him why he was walking so <u>slow</u>.
                         A   B   C   D

Answer: D. slow
The word 'so' is an adverb used to indicate a degree or extent. In this case, it is modifying another adverb. 'Slowly' would be the correct word choice.

24. The manager <u>offered</u> me a <u>fair</u> salary compared to his <u>assistant's</u>, but not as much <u>like</u> I wanted.
                      A   B   C   D

Answer: D. like
When comparing things in a positive degree, the expression is 'as…as'. The sentence should read "…but not as much <u>as</u> I wanted'.

25. <u>Even though</u> times are tough, <u>both</u> of the banks <u>gives</u> loans to <u>qualified</u> students.
         A   B   C   D

Answer: C. gives
When the word 'both' is used as the subject of a verb, it requires a plural verb. The correct word would be 'give'.

Writing Essay Answer

Writing

One essay question with 250-300 words in average

Reading passage

Political campaigns in the United States have an interesting history. At first, the candidates for president were decided by caucuses of the parties' congressional delegates. This didn't work too well because there were many abuses by party leaders. The primary elections tried to eliminate the problems of corruption.

In the primary elections, each party establishes its own rules in each state. In the beginning, each party—Republican and Democratic—gave each state two votes based on the number of electors they had in the Electoral College. (The number of members of the Electoral College has changed over time as new states were added to the United States. Currently, there are 538 votes.) The number of delegates for both parties has changed considerably over the years. In the 2016 elections, the Republican Party had 2,472 delegates, and the Democrats had 1,151. It can be complicated because each party makes its own rules about how many delegates each state will have. Some states give all of the delegates to the winner, but other states award the delegate proportionally.

Directions: Here is the transcript of a lecture.

Narrator: Now listen to part of a lecture on the topic you just read about.

Professor: Many people like to go to the national conventions. There is a lot of pageantry and high drama that goes on during the convention. The main purpose of the national political conventions is to select the person that will be the party's candidate in the presidential election. Many years ago, the political conventions were more important than they are today.

Why, do you ask, are the conventions less important? Well, because the primaries and the caucuses pretty much decide who will be nominated before the conventions begin. The conventions official role is to formally elect the candidate who will represent the party.

Some people believe that the enthusiasm shown at the nation conventions is important in getting people out to vote. Others say that party unity is strengthened in national conventions. Me, I don't know if this is necessary any more. The Internet and social media may replace the physical convention just as they have in other places in our lives.

Anyway, for now, we have national conventions that are huge, comical and fiercely debated. It is a stage for the candidate to be introduced formally to the electorate. It is also an opportunity for the party to introduce their platform. This is not a platform like an oil drilling platform, but rather a platform that is the party's stand on different issues and its principles.

Directions: You will have 20 minutes to prepare and write your response. The essay will be evaluated on how well you summarize the main points in the lecture and their connect with the reading text. Your response should be between 150 – 225 words long. You can consult the text while preparing your answer.

Summarize the main points made in the professor's talk, and explain how they contrast to the reading.

ANSWER:

Your answer should include these main points.

• Conventions today have a more ceremonial function, i.e. formally electing the presidential candidate and presenting the party platform	• Conventions were designed to choose the presidential candidate.
• The number of delegates is large and has changed over time.	• The rules for selecting the delegates is complicated, but there are more than the 538 Electoral College votes.
• Conventions are full of pageantry, high drama and humor.	• Conventions have a serious purpose, i.e. electing the presidential candidate and presenting the party platform.

Made in the USA
Lexington, KY
06 February 2018